S0-BON-980

PARTHENOPI

Books by Michael Waters

Green Ash, Red Maple, Black Gum
Bountiful
The Burden Lifters
Anniversary of the Air
Not Just Any Death
Fish Light

Editor:
Dissolve to Island: On the Poetry of John Logan
Contemporary American Poetry, Seventh Edition (with A. Poulin, Jr.)

PARTHENOPI

NEW AND SELECTED POEMS

MICHAEL WATERS

BOA Editions, Ltd.   Rochester, NY   2001

Copyright © 2001 by Michael Waters

All rights reserved
Manufactured in the United States of America

First Edition
00 01 02 03   7 6 5 4 3 2 1

Publications by BOA Editions, Ltd.—a not-for-profit corporation under section 501 (c) (3)
of the United States Internal Revenue Code—are made possible with the assistance
of grants from the Literature Program of the New York State Council on the Arts,
the Literature Program of the National Endowment for the Arts,
the Sonia Raiziss Giop Charitable Foundation,
the Eric Mathieu King Fund of The Academy of American Poets,
The Halcyon Hill Foundation, Starbucks Foundation,
as well as from the Mary S. Mulligan Charitable Trust,
the County of Monroe,and the Estate of E.M.K.

★   ★   ★

See page 186 for special individual acknowledgments.

Cover Design: Daphne Poulin-Stofer
Art: "Virgo," by Elena Zolotnitsky, courtesy of the artist.
Typesetting: Richard Foerster
Manufacturing: McNaughton & Gunn, Lithographers
BOA Logo: Mirko

Library of Congress Cataloging-in-Publication Data

Waters, Michael, 1949–
    Parthenopi : new & selected poems / Michael Waters.
        p. cm. --
    ISBN 1–880238–95–0 -- 1–880238–96–9 (pbk.)
        I. Title. II. Series.

PS3573.A818 P37 2000
811'.54--dc21

                                                                          00-057946

BOA Editions, Ltd.
Steven Huff, Publisher
Richard Garth, Chair, Board of Directors
A. Poulin, Jr., President & Founder (1976–1996)
260 East Avenue
Rochester, NY 14604
www.boaeditions.org

NATIONAL
ENDOWMENT
FOR THE ARTS

State of the Arts

NYSCA

CONTENTS

★

★

★

★

*

*

Mihaela

Te iubesc

"'And how can I go to see a delicate female with those paws?' Muniment inquired, exhibiting ten work-stained fingers.

'Buy a pair of gloves,' said Hyacinth, who recognized the serious character of this obstacle. But after a moment he added, 'No, you oughtn't to do that; she wants to see dirty hands.'"

—Henry James
The Princess Casamassima

Parthenopi

HOMO SAPIENS

Imagine a morning moon the color of cream
still steaming, a soul
newly-minted each exhalation of light,
omphalos quick with swirling aura.
Then the slow dissolve to absence.

Who can hold her?
Struck by the cold, the absolute
clarity of this nth morning of creation,
who might articulate this emotion
that somehow slipped past the masters, unnamed?

That creature whose skull was found
fragmented in lake-muck
more than one million years past her last
sigh—was she also struck by the icy
spill of moonlight so close to her cave
she might have stretched her fingers
toward its receding source?

Breasts milky in the afterglow,
she must have been beautiful, wild child,
stunned for a moment into consciousness.

The moon arcs now from that dawn to this,
passing over the bewildered
brilliance of van Gogh who brushed the moon
on thick to halt her travels,
over the unraveling intellect of Céline
who pinned the moon to a page
to prevent her passage even one night more.

But the moon forever fails over blight-scarred bark
while some early riser bears witness, fixed in the moment,
this day entered into
the log of creation by the soon-to-be forgotten
who tumble into passions
impossible to tame.

The wilderness remains with us.
The moon rises and beckons, leaving
a residue still too ancient to name.

THE STORY OF THE CAUL

When the child woke to the world,
the caul wrapping her breath
like some cheesy cloth, her
eyes filling with the billowing

clouds, the wavering gauze—
little bride, shroud-bearer—
the doctor snipped her pale
veil at the hairline,

to sell to a sailor for luck.
She remembers, she tells me now,
the mist lifting from her face,
the milky web broken,

the opalescent lights blazing back
to her kindling brain,
the shapes swimming before her
assuming flesh, more warmth,

ever more wonder—
and she closed her blue eyes
and slept, and could have been
content not to open them again.

She knows, she tells me now,
how the world begins to come true
if we stare long enough,
if we stare hard.

Be patient, Grandmother tells me.
Be still, sometimes,
to allow the numinous net of air
to mend over your face.

POLLEN

You see it as summer begins
   to shimmer on the rims
      of ponds, in rifts
         in stone where ants assume
their awesome responsibilities,
     on eaves of Victorian mansions
      limned with last light—
        pale curtains sweeping
among the generous trees,
    messages sent between green
     families, greetings
       before the heat strikes us
too lazy to speak, or even
    nod in the sullen breeze,
      surging across the vast
        expanses of lawns, past
new screens, tumbling
   through rich stories of air
     to dust floors, mirrors,
       every surface with a frail
film where a boy can trace
   his name, then raise
     the finger to his lips
      to taste the feathery
light, the bright ash, the yellow
   powder etching the whorls
     of his finger's tip with mild
      fire, incandescence,

this swollen glimmer, loose
spirit, the hours' aura,
the plush, allusive
tremble of pollen.

READING DICKENS

Not long after the war, my father
   bought, by mail, the complete set
      of the works of Charles Dickens,

each book bound in black and red
   imitation leather, the titles
      embossed in gold.

The set filled a small bookcase
   near an overstuffed chair
      where my father spent

languid evenings in lamplight,
   feet propped on the hassock,
      while David Copperfield

and honest Nicholas Nickleby
   fought their unsure way
      through a wicked world.

He might have imagined me,
   his only son, not yet born,
      on his lap, learning to read.

Each time he finished a book,
   he slipped a dollar
      between the gilt-edged pages—

some nights, the money low,
   he and my mother bounced
      before the bookcase, shaking

each volume, the few bills
  falling, enough for dinner
    or the double feature.

Decades later, reading Dickens,
  I imagine those early years,
    their slow stroll home,

her arm circling his waist,
  the whistling, papery leaves,
    the bath she drew before bed

while he waited downstairs, reading
  Dickens, happy not to be
    living some great adventure,

happy to close the book
  before my mother slept,
    saving the ending for tomorrow.

HORSE

The first horse I ever saw
   was hauling a wagon stacked with furniture
      past storefronts along Knickerbocker Avenue.
He was taller than a car, blue-black with flies,

and bits of green ribbon tied to his mane
   bounced near his caked and rheumy eyes.
      I had seen horses in books before, but
this horse shimmered in the Brooklyn noon.

I could hear his hooves strike the tar,
   the colossal nostrils snort back the heat,
      and breathe his inexorable, dung-tinged fume.
Under the enormous belly, his ——

swung like the policeman's nightstick,
   a dowsing rod, longer than my arm—
      even the Catholic girls could see it
hung there like a rubber spigot.

When he let loose, the steaming street
   flowed with frothy, spattering urine.
      And when he stopped to let the junkman
toss a tabletop onto the wagon bed,

I worked behind his triangular head
   to touch his foreleg above the knee,
      the muscle jerking the mat of hair.
Horse, I remember thinking,

four years old and standing there,
   struck momentarily dumb,
      while the power gathered in his thigh
surged like language into my thumb.

COVERT STREET

The boy who lived in the library
slept among the stacks, behind long rows
of reference, awakening now and then to peek
from a gap in the book-bricked wall, one eye

gleaming across the marble floors or
his paste-scented breath feathering my neck
where I stood choosing three books from the profusion
ranging the stained and oaken shelves.

Three books were all the librarian would allow
a boy to carry home, only three
fingered from the festooned section for Young Readers,
yellow streamers framing their glossy spines.

I'd spend hours browsing those books, frowning
like the Hasidic fathers who suffered endless rounds
of chess in the park, rocking my bent body back
and forth till I finally made my choice.

I took my time because I loved the silence,
the scrubbed, glimmering aisles, the smell of lemon wax,
and the dust motes drifting through pillars of light
like snow through synagogue windows in the Carpathians.

A boy could breathe there, and never be bored.
He could learn to love his mother, those mournful
vowels, and his father, the harsh consonants,
then tender their names in a luminous language.

He could leave the library, as I did, as twilight
deepened, to begin the familiar walk home
with three books bracing his arm,
and count off each street, those eternal,

Brooklyn blocks he'd never forget
—Hancock, Halsey, Eldert—, then pause
when he came to his own, Covert Street
hushed in the breeze bowing the sycamores.

THE MYSTERY OF THE CAVES

I don't remember the name of the story,
but the hero, a boy, was lost,
wandering a labyrinth of caverns
filling stratum by stratum with water.

I was wondering what might happen:
would he float upward toward light?
Or would he somersault forever
in an underground black river?

I couldn't stop reading the book
because I had to know the answer,
because my mother was leaving again—
the lid of the trunk thrown open,

blouses torn from their hangers,
the crazy shouting among rooms.
The boy found it impossible to see
which passage led to safety.

One yellow finger of flame
wavered on his last match.
There was a blur of perfume—
Mother breaking miniature bottles,

then my father gripping her,
but too tightly, by both arms.
The boy wasn't able to breathe.
I think he wanted me to help,

but I was small, and it was late.
And my mother was sobbing now,
no longer cursing her life,
repeating my father's name

among bright islands of skirts
circling the rim of the bed.
I can't recall the whole story,
what happened at the end. . . .

Sometimes I worry that the boy
is still searching below the earth
for a thin pencil of light,
that I can almost hear him

through great volumes of water,
through centuries of stone,
crying my name among blind fish,
wanting so much to come home.

LIPSTICK

Who can hurry past the five-and-dime,
the cardboard Max Factor ad

fading in the yellow light
of the abandoned, fly-littered window,

without recognizing the miniature skyline—
spires, smokestacks, the blinking, red antennae—

his mother's lipsticks etched
on the powdered, greenhouse air of her bedroom?

Only God or someone taller could count them!
I wanted to explore that foreign city,

hold her hand across the cinnabar avenues,
whisper in libraries of peach frost and ruby.

Grey school-mornings in the railroad flat,
pretending to be still asleep,

I'd watch my mother dress
for the subway ride into Manhattan.

She'd sit in her bra and half-slip,
elbows propped on the vanity top,

brushing flames across her lips,
first one flavor, then another—

forbidden strawberry, crushed orange, café au lait—
then close her lips on a tissue.

I'd steal the paper from the wicker
basket to taste the exotic

spices, the delicious
mocha, crème caramel, glazed papaya,

and when I was older, ten or twelve,
I'd wrap tissue after tissue

around my small, preening member,
smudging the lipstick on my flesh.

I never wrestled any desire
to smear the lipstick on my face,

touch the tubes
to my own parched lips,

but was touched by the story of Rilke,
poor Rainer, whose suffocating mother

painted the lips of her dear Maria!
O the poems! His problems with women!

Was his mother drawing out,
as she layered shade upon shade,

the lovely woman who lived inside him,
or was she blotting out,

dyeing his lips a deeper red, deeper
till almost black,

the boy who peeked
from behind his eyelids, feverish and weak?

SINGING FOR ELIZABETH

How often have I tried to please you,
tracing your passage down Covert Street
where you floated, tenement goddess,
blown hair brushing the cypress branches,

floated with the joyful ease of the unborn,
raising my name to the Brooklyn rooftops,
calling to me among scorched tires and debris
that we might compare our inchoate desires?

My secret was the yearning, singular boyhood
I kept hidden, bruised marble, in my pocket.
Why should I have hurt you, imaginary twin,
made known that I slipped into this world alone?

That twelfth summer we wandered arm-in-arm,
counting couples in the abandoned schoolyard,
past the shattered mothers of the shoelace factory,
till you began to dissolve in the bell-struck breeze,

in the wishful dreaming, Elizabeth, gentle sister
who once touched your lips to my ear
to whisper: *Offer your solitude a name,*
then sing to her down the trash-lit alleys of air.

SHADOW BOXES

in memoriam Joseph Cornell

*"The intense longing to get into the boxes this overflow-
ing, a richness & poetry felt when working . . ."*

Six A.M. I'd be walking those sycamore-
   lined streets alone, red rubber
     ball in one hand, sawed-off

broomstick on my shoulder, waiting
   for a few friends to rise, morning
     to commence among parked cars

and manhole covers, the sun looming
   at last above tenement rooftops
     crisscrossed with clotheslines.

His slanted cellar-door would be propped
   open and I'd step down, eyes
     adjusting to the low

wattage, into the enormous clutter
   of his workshop, tables strewn with wire,
     paint-slick slats of wood, severed

dolls' heads, porcelain pipes, thimbles,
   tiny stoppered bottles cleansed
     of lapsed medicines,

birds' nests, children's building-blocks,
   their letters sandpapered off,
     brass rings, ticket stubs, magazines—

the magazines!—tossed everywhere, 1940s
   illustrated ladies' weeklies, *National*
      Geographics, U.S. Army manuals,

storybooks and road atlases and astronomical
   charts, greeting cards bought
      bulk in boxes from thrift shops,

this world so dense with detail
   and populated with such familiar
      yet somehow exotic bric-a-brac

I'd forget I was below the thronged
   avenues of Flushing, 1964, my friends
      running bases on Utopia Parkway.

For hours I'd sit on a high stool
   with long scissors, turning pages,
      carefully clipping pictures—

parrots, Medici princes, even Lauren Bacall—
   while he pasted them in boxes
      of his own devising, concentrating

on each particular shade of blue, or
   the shape the paper made
      against a backdrop of winter stars,

but this morning he stopped, staring
   into the wreckage for something—
      he wasn't conscious of what—

until his glance chanced upon a ball
   balanced on a Coca-Cola bottle,
      and before I had the chance

to say *Wait, it's mine*, he'd placed it—
    just so—on two thin wires
        suspended over wineglasses, each

filled with a milky-blue cat's-eye marble,
    and now we were done for the day,
        at ease, sipping seltzer

before I returned to stifling streets
    oddly empty, monochromatic,
        lacking a certain delicacy

and playfulness, a world taken too
    seriously in sunlight, intent
        upon its own inviolability

as my eyes half-closed to glare
    slashing off fenders and hoods
        freshly washed and waxed

and buffed a metallic blue, but still
    not the blue that blazed
        below the earth, in darkness,

in a world where nothing would be lost,
    where everything was given purpose,
        if only it could remain patient.

MYTHOLOGY

Because no one has ever asked,
because the task is incumbent upon me,
I want to reveal the secret
gathering place of heroes:

we scaled the rough, stucco wall
of a row of one-story garages
and loitered on the tar roof,
staring down the weakening sun—

Tommy O'Brien, Glenn Marshall,
everyone's girl, Rosemarie Angelastro,
and the dumb kid, Gregory Galunas,
who let ants walk on his tongue.

We smoked butts and told no one.
Once Billy McAssey jumped
and stove the canvas top
of a cream-and-blue convertible.

At five o'clock the mothers
groaned their chorus from the curb,
each name shouted like a warning
to the worn men leaving work.

But I remained on the roof
till lights blinked on in tenements,
the smell of fish oiled the air,
and radios sent forth tinny polkas . . .

and through a tinted wing of glass
began to read the heavens,
the bright syllables of stars,
as words took shape, lyrical prose,

a whole story
filled with heroes, their great names,
their impending deaths praised
on the darkening pages of the sky.

A smart kid,
when I asked my spiritless father,
"Where do the dead go?"
I already knew the answer.

THE CONVERSION OF SAINT PAUL

In 1956 I was the shepherd boy
with nothing to offer the infant Jesus.

Kissed goodbye, I left the walk-up
in a white, ankle-length, terrycloth robe,

flailing my grandfather's wooden cane
wrapped from crook to tip in foil.

Secretaries stared from passing buses
at this Biblical apparition

leading his invisible sheep to school,
O little, wild-eyed prophet of Brooklyn!

Older, I portrayed the leper
gifted with half of St. Martin's cloak

and, with paper arrows and red Play-Doh,
evoked the passion of St. Sebastian.

Then I had to fake a terrible fall
to honor the conversion of St. Paul—

when I changed into costume
in the boys' musty coatroom,

Sister Euphrasia knelt to hike
the elastic waistband of my briefs

to better arrange my torn-sheet toga.
In second grade, this ageless ogre

had pasted Easter seals on my skull
and locked me in a cobwebbed cubicle,

pretending to air-mail me to China
where I'd never again see my mother!

Funny enough today, I guess,
but then I pleaded for forgiveness.

Now her sour breath flushed my face
when—classmates clamoring their impatience—

she whispered Jesus
would be judging my performance,

then thrust me from her failing sight
to be apprehended by all that light.

CHRIST AT THE APOLLO, 1962

"Even in religious fervor there is a touch of animal heat."
—Walt Whitman

Despite the grisly wounds portrayed in prints,
the ropy prongs of blood stapling His eyes
or holes like burnt half-dollars in His feet,
the purple gash a coked teenybopper's
lipsticked mouth in His side, Christ's suffering
seemed less divine than the doubling-over
pain possessing "the hardest working man."
I still don't know whose wounds were worse: Christ's brow
thumbtacked with thorns, humped crowns of feet spike-split—
or James Brown's shattered knees. It's blasphemy
to equate such ravers in their lonesome
afflictions, but when James collapsed on stage
and whispered *please please please*, I rocked with cold,
forsaken Jesus in Gethsemane
and, for the first time, grasped His agony.
Both rose, Christ in His unbleached muslin gown
to assume His rightful, heavenly throne,
James wrapped in his cape, pussy-pink satin,
to ecstatic whoops of fans in Harlem.
When resurrection tugs, I'd rather let
The Famous Flames clasp my hand to guide me
than proud Mary or angelic orders
still befuddled by unbridled passion.
Pale sisters foisted relics upon me,
charred splinter from that chatty thief's cross and
snipped thread from the shroud that xeroxed Christ's corpse,
so I can't help but fashion the future—

soul-struck pilgrims prostrate at the altar
that preserves our Godfather's three-inch heels
or, under glass, like St. Catherine's skull, *please*,
his wicked, marcelled conk, his tortured knees.

DEMONSTRATION:
WOMEN'S HOUSE OF DETENTION, 1965

---

demolished 1973-74
in memoriam JL
d. 1980

Blood-inked political leaflets pelted Village streets,
a revamped Biblical plague,
the stringed, sodden, menses-red confetti of the damned
delivered upon tourists
thronging the annual sidewalk art exhibition,
unshaven sunglass'd Sunday
bohemians sporting Bermuda shorts and sandals,
sidestepping spontaneous
abstract splatters, the city's interactive canvas,
as blasphemous breezes arced
Sixth Avenue, the cries of revolutionary
angels celebrating ruin
as the quickening, laval ash smudged our doomed island.
I stared up at barred windows
as flame-licked hands emerged to launch sleek kamikaze
Paracletes, fourteen stories
suffused with curses and filth and rancorous laughter.
"Don't listen!" warned my mother
as we navigated Manhattan's hewn passages,
fleeing into a bookshop
off MacDougal—refuge from the clotted tongues of rain—
where Mother purchased for me
a slender volume of hip, nonsensical fables
whose author, the "smart" Beatle,
would be gunned down uptown from the siren-spooked wreckage,

the lascivious ghost-site
of stumped adolescence, the helter-skelter, holy,
fallen
     Women's House of D.

THE '66 METS

The el rattled past the Unisphere, skeletal,
the gristly webbing of some sea creature
left to bleach in the industrial
rain of Queens. The World's Fair was over.
The game called, we were thrown together
hip-to-hip to convey the deep
disinterest of commuters in one another's
lives, staring hard into the abandoned
thoroughfares of the future, not speaking.
But breathing. And one fan sidled up
to nestle his mouth in my hair, his beery
breath swabbing one ear, stiff prick
pressed into the damp hollow of my back,
passengers packed around us, yet distant,
a crowd in a photograph, the couplings
not clear.
            Until a small commotion broke
out, some guy with two boys in baseball
gear clinging to his belt
warning, *Back off, bud*, his palm against
the breather's chest, the onlookers
tense but making room as the express
drummed into Queens Plaza and the amateur
molester ghosted off into the gray,
steel anonymity of the girders.
                              Fifteen,
I was too dumbstruck to murmur thanks, still
too simple to grasp how desire
can bully the body, any body, that father
ashen too, knuckling his boys' bristly
scalps beneath their blue caps

as the doors hissed shut and the train
jerked away from the station
into the spattering April
drizzle, an outcry of sparks
bursting from under blunt wheels,
the long, frustrating season just begun.

STONING THE BIRDS

How can any bird-hunting boy know the low passages
   through the thorned and knotted brambles
     till he veers off the horse trail
to startle some couple lovemaking among the pines,

her yessing head haloed with gnats as his back
   sweeps their splintery bed of brown
     needles, tongues looping their vague
script upon sky? I swayed near the thicket,

fingering pocketfuls of stones, till she stopped
   oaring the air to glance at me, register
     my familiar, acned face, then shrug
back to her sleepy summer pleasure. What did I matter,

one goofy teenager dumbstruck in khaki shorts,
   as he bucked and she bounced, then
     unglued herself from his glistening,
slug-slick stump? I finally jolted awake enough

to sneaker back the path to Twin Mountains Manor
   where my bent father swept long-legged
     spiders off the shuffleboard court
and my mother staggered the stiff-backed

Adirondack chairs into rows for spectators.
   I dawdled till the sinners sidled
     among us, staring hard for any sign
of dark complicity, tick-ridden consciences,

ash streaking her temple or sulphur slitting
  his eyes, as he chalked his name, *Benny*,
    onto the scoreboard, then toed the line.
What did I know about the fall of sunlight and shade

that slow June afternoon as my skinny buddies
  cannonballed from the low board, as Benny
    skimmed the puck toward the inverted
pyramid and all his proud sisters squealed?

I clumped up the knoll to the kiddie-loud
  pool and dove, wishing I could remain
    underwater till summer was over,
hold my breath till the planet stopped whirling

long enough for me to grasp it with cupped hands,
  press it against my cheek to measure
    the snared pulse—poor stunned jay—then
shovel it back into blue air and watch it flicker away.

AMONG BLACKBERRIES

Her lips blue from tasting, her eyes so blue,
she stares at the boy on the bicycle
who stares at her breasts
through the thin, cotton blouse.

I was fourteen and didn't know
our lives come down to moments
forgotten
until so many miles later, perhaps

stuck in the slow bloom of traffic,
the sun pressing its memory
into thighs . . . the horns
blare us back from another country

where I have been bicycling again
among hills, among blackberries.
Noon strikes its dumb chord
through the part in my pale hair.

I stop pedaling now to stare—
her lips blue from tasting, eyes so blue,
the struck moment of her breasts,
the blackberries sweating in their bucket.

THE SCENT OF APPLES

One morning, waking
to the fresh scent of apples,
their sweet breath
pearling the curtains with moisture,

I rose to gather the small, red mouths
scattered across the lawn.
Someone, a bum, paused each night
below our windows and stars,

snapping apples from the tree—
he peeled each one perfectly,
then tossed the skins,
curving and whole, onto the grass.

I placed them in jars
filled with rainwater and cloves,
and would not sleep one summer
until I heard the blade

sliding under his thumb,
loosening the thin, red dress,
until the scent of apples
rose to my nostrils like sex,

and those ripe mouths, blossoming,
promised everything.

The boy rehearsing the Continental Stroll
before the mirror in his bedroom—
does he memorize the sweep of hair
tumbling across his eyes
when he spins once, then claps his hands?

Home from school in winter,
he studies the couples on television,
their melancholy largo,
how they glide together, then separate.
Such dancing makes him nervous—
so many hand motions to remember,
where to slide his feet, plus
every girl in the gym staring at him.

That boy was familiar, twenty years ago,
saying hello to a loneliness
peculiar to the tender,
                              the high-strung
lanterns suspended above the dance floor,
ousting shadows, leaving him
more alone, trapped in the spotlight.

The Peppermint Twist, The Bristol Stomp,
The Hully Gully are only memory,
but loneliness still dances
among the anxious ghosts of the heart,
preparing to stroll
down a line formed by teenagers

mouthing lyrics, clapping hands,
forever awkward,
each partner dreaming of grace.

THE DIFFERENCE BETWEEN A ROOSTER
AND A WHORE

Those adolescent jokes blown from mouth
　　to sour mouth, that sham
　　　resuscitation, the snickering
　　　　gusts through schoolyards,
nudges and leers when the girls
　　breezed by—are they still making
　　　their slow rounds, winding
　　　　their way back to us, unchanged?
When I paused in the anonymous
　　snow to piss obscenities
　　　in looping script, did I scrawl
　　　　my name in the devil's book?
Last week on a crosstown bus
　　a woman's umbrella snagged
　　　her skirt, the wire tugging
　　　　toward mid-thigh. The driver,
glancing in the mirror, grinned
　　at me, his bawdy buddy.
　　　Any cock'll do, the kids
　　　　crowed, stoned on the pier
those sultry nights, gulping
　　beer and shaking their cans
　　　to tease the hushed
　　　　girls' hair with spray—
then hammered some fisherman's
　　slimy haul: gasping eels,
　　　garbage fish, the frothing,
　　　　vulgar mouth of the stingray.

SCOTCH AND SUN

Home from night shift, my father
was too wired from fighting warehouse fires
to sleep—so he'd sip several Dewar's,
then rouse me for a morning at the beach.
There the combination of scotch and sun
would knock him out for a couple hours
while I invented tasks near the breakage—
skimming clam shells, counting one-legged gulls—
till he woke to hoist me onto his shoulders
and march into the sea, deeper with each step.
He'd look down to find a boy propped there,
his blazing, acceptable burden, his crown, almost
an abstraction shimmering from his skull,
some image of himself he once believed he'd been.
Then arch his neck to shut away the glare.
That noon I leaned too far back, back until my head
dipped into the combers, then below. . .
I struggled, thrashing my legs,
but my father clasped them tighter, closer
to his chest, oblivious, and went on
breasting the rollers, teasing the undertow.
Those broad shoulders eclipsed the sun.
Then hands grasped my hair—I was choking—
while my startled father stammered excuses
to the impromptu chorus of gawking bathers.
He was more surprised than I, more scared.
He shook when he told my furious mother.
I simply had no idea, he said. Jesus,
that boy almost drowned
though I held him in my arms.

BROOKLYN WATERFALL

Water where you least expect it:
  swelling every closet,
    tumbling down stairwells,

raining through light
  fixtures onto night tables . . .
    my good Aunt Beatrice,

ever forgetful, had twisted
  the faucet handle fully,
    plugging the drain

with a red rubber stopper,
  then set off to shop.
    If water can be joyous,

imagine the unfettered
  revelry: no one home,
    the glorious, porcelain

plashing from the third
  story so loud, abandoned,
    anticipatory.

By the time she piddled
  Saturday morning away,
    the water had traveled

miles—no slow, molten
  flow, but unabashed
    raveling, elemental motion.

So when my aunt looked up
    from her swollen mop,
        my father stormed back out,

the water trailing him
    to the local tavern.
        He swilled it with bourbon.

How far he managed to float away
    from his fearful, weeping family,
        or for how many hours,

I don't remember, but
    he swayed home later,
        muttered *what the hell*,

and joined the communal
    sweeping, work that keeps
        a family together, water

still seeping into the earth
    where it waits for us,
        not needing forgiveness.

APPLES

for my father

I was the clumsy child
who stole apples
from your favorite tree
to toss them into the lake.

I have no excuse, but
those apples were never lost.
Each night, while you slept,
as apples bobbed in moonlight,

I waited in shallow water
until the apples washed ashore.
Each night I gave you an apple.
Sometimes I remember that desire

to take whatever belongs to you
so I can return it.
Now, on windless nights,
when the lake lies still,

I have another dream:
I gather you in my arms,
after death, and ease you
like a basketful of apples

into the moonlit water,
and we float home,
with an awkward grace,
to a continent dark with apples.

WASPS

for my father

Dead C battery, souvenir lighter, spool minus thread,
lipstick tube lacking a smudge of red:
we'd rummage junk drawers to fill the squares.
But the lost chessmen?—
they click against glass, black
bishops bidding me open the window,
wheedling a wary God to release them
to crusade for their king gone ahead to Jerusalem.

LAST JOKE

"Mike's not gonna like it," my mother warned
in nervous, perpetual undersong,
but he blundered forward, slurring the one
about high-tech robots swarming the course—
caddies, groundskeepers, roving bartenders—,
the club members pleased, but then complaining
when the glare off tin torsos spoiled their scores.
"So they painted them black," he couldn't stop—
I could see what was coming, almost flinched,
while my mother scoured my kitchen basin,
hoping to avoid some loveless display,
the return to our hushed, prickly routine—
"and next day seven of them phoned in sick."
He stood scrappy, blunt as oak, sore loser,
knowing I'd voted for Clinton, for "choice,"
for lifting the ban on queers in foxholes,
the idea of some kid not unlike me
fixing the unbroken economy
rubbing him raw. "Dad," I growled, "not funny."
Who could have guessed this joke would be his last?—
not that watery, offensive punch line,
but his classic, bug-eyed zinger—*Gotcha!*—
as I chipped more ice into his Dewar's,
charmed by the flawless, cornball delivery.
"Pit bulls," sputtered my mother, letting go
the steel wool. We seeded our half-acre,
scorched scrub lawn, tramped combed furrows till his heart
hammered him home, and wasn't my mother
right? I didn't like it, but didn't flinch—
not from those black robots, their unforeseen
consequences, nor from the crude, helpless

humor of my father who taught me how
to spread just enough shit upon this green,
incorrect, forever dying planet.

BLACK LEAVES

Once, in a field,
in the black shade of an oak,
an open coffin filling with leaves. . . .

You want to sleep there forever,
surrounded by crickets
coaxing their sad, imaginary violins.

Say it's Sunday, the sky gone
white with staring. All morning
you've imagined nothing but heat,

the slow pressure of perspiration
on your wrist. You might start counting
sparrows confused in the valley,

but the coffin interrupts your romance
like a mother. So you circle
twice, making sure

there's been no mistake. Perhaps
this coffin belongs to your neighbor.
Perhaps it arrived by mail

years ago, was lost in revival,
abandoned in the cellar like preserves.
But the heat is blossoming, there's

too much to think, the red silk
rustles like cool water & the leaves,
the black leaves,

are falling one by one
until you can no longer resist, so
you slip in & sleep like . . . nothing at all.

PRESERVES

I found the preserves in the cellar,
canned decades ago
by the woman who brought this house
on wheels from Missouri.

The black raspberries were still
delicious, each cluster
burning like years in the brain.
I could almost hear the song

used to press those raspberries
into jars thinner, now, than dust,
almost imitate each gesture
as the stain rose on my fingers.

The stuffed owls are crumbling now
like rags left too long in bins,
the black rafters warp,
but the slow spirals of dust

still resist sweeping,
having been written in the journal
of the lost, to keep track
of what passes, what preserves.

FOUNDLING

girl with marsh fever, 1824

I was born in the mouth of a bull,
my sisters tell me. I see him now,
an immense, black presence, commanding
the lilies of his field, the littlest blooms
swaying with awe among the ragged grasses.
His eye is large and liquid, the world
rounded there, and kept distant.
His lip is thick as the bow of a boat.
When I have been kissed goodnight,
the scarlet kerchief knotting my throat,
my family whispering near the fire,
I can recall the flax of his tongue,
the hand-me-down bunting of his breath,
the crooked slats of teeth: my crib.
My father was seeding furrows
when an infant's cry shrilled forth,
a song of innocence. Steaming nostrils.
And I was taken from that paludal hutch.
I was born in the mouth of a bull,
a fragile, extraordinary girl—
some ancient book holds a prophecy
I must be meant to fulfill.

CHRISOMS

early 19th C

Impossible curls fluorescing like aurorae,
  salmon limbs almost bursting with fat,
    they float in some ecclesiastical ether
  within cracked tondi darkened with rot.
God smiles upon them, and each smiles back.
  Smallpox, influenza, whooping cough, pleurisy,
    the simple wasting away in that snow-struck
  century—yet who's more joyous than twelve
chrisoms still swaddled in birth-clouds,
  the baptismal frocks that rendered them
    legless, half-spirit, while propped
  in doll-sized coffins, shed now as they rush
across the broad-brushed sky? Pure flesh
  lends symmetry: hibiscus buds of penises,
    the creamy, vaginal erasures
  babe-sweet, nimbus-wisped, incorruptible.
Good artists loathed them, so painted them
  with ferocity. Not one looks real, though.
    Not one seems the object of compassion
  or, for all such pious preening, envy.
While these dead daughters and sons remain
  perfect, ascendant, the planet
    still swerves, avoiding the sun.
  Chrisoms swarm the plains and beckon.
When we squint to name them, they're gone again.

BURNING THE DOLLS

*In 1851, in John Humphrey Noyes' free-love settlement
in Oneida, New York, the communally-raised children,
encouraged by the adults, voted to burn their dolls as
representative of the traditional role of motherhood.*

That last night, unable to sleep,
   I prayed with my doll
      under the twisted-star
quilt, then held her close,

her flannel gown warming my cheek,
   her hair made of yarn
      brushing the tears away.
I sang her favorite lullaby,

then she sang it back to me.
   When the sky flared into dawn
      I carried her in my arm—
not crying now for anyone to see—

to my sisters barefoot on the lawn,
   circling the stacked wood, each
      bearing some small body
that stared into the remote sun.

And when the burning was done,
   when her white, Sunday dress
      was transformed to ash
and each perfect, grasping

finger melted upon the coals,
    when her varnished face burst
        in the furnace of my soul,
the waxy lips forever lost,

then I knew I'd no longer pray,
    even with fire haunting me,
        because I hadn't resembled
closely enough my mother,

hadn't withheld my burgeoning
    desire, so like a doll
        concealing what I'd learned
I burned and burned and burned.

THOSE ALTERNATE SUNDAYS

when my daughter's tugged
   home—diminishing yellow skull
      a balloon blown beyond the western

pond—, the raspberry tang of shampoo
   seeps into pillows and futon;
      her tuneless whistle needles the hall;

the torn, lacy hem of her soul
   nestles among Victorian dolls
      strung in hammocks along one wall.

Porcelain faces press bright webbing.
   Come here, I beckon the leaf-wisp . . .
      Come down, I urge, as if tempting

a hummingbird with a fingertip's
   blister of nectar . . . and when
      I exhaust myself and sleep,

the summoned transparency
   burgeons, puffing the rumpled
      bed's canopy, then softening

the wintry pane with our common
   breath, willing my daughter to return
      to murmur her secret name.

                    for Kiernan

THE CURIOSITIES

Medical Museum
Walter Reed Hospital

One jar stamped "what remains of the brain of Charles Guiteau"
& wedged among larger jars of pale microcephalics—
bug-eyed incubi squatting on sleepers in fairy-tale illustrations—
glints in the fluorescence. Stillborn
cyclops, syphilitic penises like blanched stalks of angelica,
the head of a young seaman flowering with red algae—
how would Whitman have catalogued this library
as he browsed hand in hand with his brakeman
among the singular stacks? Could his unshakable love
for the disinherited and homesick and gangrenous
teenage privates embrace these fused twins, their incestuous
union, face-trunk-crotch merging vertically
into crotch-trunk-face, blunt arms
radiating, little human starfish? My own lover
stares, rapt, at the stitched lips of these spongy children
who stare back from their brackish
cradle through decades of dust. Blistery nights,
as she twists in sleep, I'll slip off the sheet
& draw my fingers over her damp,
imperfect breasts till the dawn seeps outward,
till desire flares. How then can I forget
these jars stuffed with the invisible
masses who touch us in our dreams, who steep
our yearnings in their milky waters?—suspended
curiosities, terrible beauties, hushed assassins.

THE BLIND

He might be changing the tire on the pickup
when he notices the life there:
something blunt, luminous,
struggling in the earth in the tread . . .

and he might swallow his last beer
and wonder at the lives we lead,
so blind, caught
"in the turning wheel of the universe."

*

And don't we all have friends
lost in tragedy,
the man who backed his pickup
over his own daughter, who
refuses to touch another wheel forever?

*

Until one Sunday he decides it's time,
so he opens the garage doors
like the Book of the Dead,
charges the battery,
then backs, carefully, into sunlight . . .

where the truck still looks familiar
as the runaway dog
come home with three good legs,
and the engine turns over and over
with abandon, and the radio

pulls the whole world into the cool
cab, but it isn't enough . . .

the flat road stretches for miles
in all directions, one tire
still wobbles, so
the tools must be gathered,
and the beer. . . .

*

By now the stars begin to appear,
one by one, till the sky's
chalked with messages.

He'll read them before dawn.

But tonight, for a few moments,
the glare of his cigarette
punctuating heaven's final sentence,
he stares into his cupped palm,
into the red
earth . . .

*

because something is moving there,
because it's blind,

because he wants to make sure
it lives through the night.

YELLOW STARS

*Starting on April 29, 1942, the Dutch Jews
were forced to wear a yellow Star of David.*

Crossing the Prinsengracht canal
  from the greengrocers' shops
    to the bookstalls and cafés,

grasping my mother's hand,
  the water below sweeping
    winter's debris to the sea,

I spotted three yellow stars
  bicycling toward me, fallen,
    I guess, from the sky.

I gazed through layers of air—
  daylight, but I could tell
    the stars were no longer there.

Later I saw yellow stars
  everywhere: on trams, swaying
    to Wagner in the park,

yellow stars trying to feel
  at home, hovering over
    little stars, their children.

But soon the stars floated
  away, puffs of smoke
    over the opening fields,

the icy blossoms of jasmine.
　　Then winter again, our flowers
　　　gone, the stars vanished.

Where did the yellow stars go?
　　Do you, like me, long to know,
　　　staring into the night

sky to search among the white,
　　thermal stars, the flaring
　　　orange, for those few

yellow stars that returned
　　home, that call down now
　　　to this strange planet:

behold us in the milky
　　light of creation
　　　waiting to be born

IN MEMORY OF SMOKE

I found her again this morning,
my mother, sleeping
with her head in the oven,
on a pillow of human hair.

On her knees, exhausted,
wanting the oven forever clean,
she might have been praying
in memory of smoke.

I don't know her reasons.
I guess something simple
as cleaning the oven
becomes a compulsion for those

who have been lost in snow,
in childhood, wandering
from town to burning town
in search of a family.

I guess you might recognize
the family as smoke
billowing over black trees.
So I let my mother sleep.

I know she would never shut
her eyes, place her cheek
on the burning pillow each night,
without a prayer for her family,

giving thanks
for the work she manages daily,
in memory of smoke,
in fear of the coming snow.

THE BROOCH

Some cruel entrepreneur glued jewels onto wings
to prevent their broad, papery flowering,
the ruby or sapphire or smoky opal hump
wedged in an oval frame, its frail gold chain
blunted with a pin, so the exotic beetle,
living brooch, could plod its strict loop.
Pinned to my mother's monogrammed blouse,
that insect circled her initial, *D*, endlessly,
one arm of a clock wild with sprung tension,
symbol of *time passing* in early Bergman.
Then Mother cushioned a fish bowl with confetti,
the exiled prince plush in his glass palace,
and though she sprinkled water and crushed matzoh,
the beetle soon rocked onto its burdened back.
For days it lay among shredded funnies
because she couldn't bear to pry the jewel
from the sleek carapace, snap the foreign skull,
couldn't touch the withered roach.
No one spoke its brittle, miniature corpse.
Then Grandmother, in her gruff, Old World manner,
crumbled what remained of that conversation piece
into soot, the blue-black powder backdrop now
for the gem that flamed in her furrowed palm:
her stuck-in-the-throat history of sifting ash
from unearthed sancta of charred flesh
till clasping one daughter's heirloom brooch.

ANNIVERSARY OF THE AIR

Past storefronts lit among the dusk-swept avenues
where those broken grandmothers spit
or straighten their babushkas in the smoky light
   of sausages, streaked windows
hung with strings of red and green peppers,
bluefish gazing through galaxies of pink glaze,

she groans up the bursting, rubble-strewn path
where Our Lady of the Ascension
glistens in rain—
to light one candle, by habit, for her husband
who no longer rests, even in memory,
with any detail,

though tonight she might remember his hair,
red as the candle, or
his alert, political mind flickering
like the flame on its black wick.

The seraphic coloratura of the choir
lulls her. . . .

She'll hear them later, distinct, bordering
   her bed, cold water
whispering through the walls, whispering
her name—*Anna*—across the vast
privacies of so many years

so that, in sleep, those tongues start to storm
   through her breast and cross the narrows
   of her lips,
cries of homesickness overwhelming the vermilion
   sky of her arrival,
cries of wrenching in bone-weary orgasm mixed
   with the animal cries of her husband,
cries of her daughters awash in the headlights
   of automobiles racing the rose-blown
   wallpaper (or were those her cries too?),
old-language cries across back alleys
   of rug-beatings and boiling laundry,

the last cries transforming into birdsong
   in the crenellated dawn
as she awakens, light-struck, this swallow
   of a woman, to celebrate the past,
   this anniversary of the air
issuing forth
with the now-recalled memory of his hair:

yes, *red*, and for this anniversary—
with thanksgiving to Our Lady—
the color is enough.

FRANK SINATRA

I love to listen to men in bars,
the lonely drinkers

who finger their last ice-cubes
until frost surrounds the skin
like a wedding ring,

who hum softly to themselves
tunes popular decades ago,

whose wives sweat through sleep
in rooms only streetlights away.

*

Every drunk thinks he's Frank Sinatra

and each bored husband has a story
that has nothing to do
with the worn face mooning
above the bottles into the mirror,

but the story touches you
like the man who hopes to bum a drink.

*

One night some guy showed me his hands—
swollen, humped with scar-tissue,
navy-blue at the knuckles.

Those hands had done everything—
fought in the Golden Gloves,
hauled barrels of nails,
patted the ass, once, of Lana Turner.

He told me his bare right hand
had driven nails into bar-tops . . .

*

and he took a nail from his pocket
and, for whiskey,
raised his palm above my eyebrows,
then brought it down, *hard*,
onto the flecked & ragged head. . . .

*

I won't tell you what happened,
but after several beers,
after the ballgame flickered off,
that man began to sing,
loud enough for everyone to hear . . .

Hello, young lovers, whoever you are
I hope your troubles are few. . .

and soon other men stopped drumming
their tables with fingertips,
stopped lifting their glasses,
their miserable swizzle
sticks. . . .

*

His voice swept onto the street
and maybe his wife slept on . . .

dreaming of that night, years ago,
when she & her handsome young sailor
held hands in the balcony
of the Paramount

where Frank Sinatra sang
only for them.

MONOPOLY

The loneliness of two people
together, rolling dice
as if their luck might change,
arrives with the breeze

of moths fanning a lampshade,
casual, without voice—
so the radio keeps reciting
those brokenhearted syllables

that tumble through the open
window onto the wet street.
When I glance up, I can see
the woman dancing, alone,

while her husband swaps deeds,
steers a miniature, silver
racer along the boardwalk
or, worse, drags a worn shoe

onto Baltic Avenue, past peep-shows
where couples simulate sex
on screens flecked with grime.
This game seems crazy to her

because its holds the boredom
back only a few minutes, because
no one can possess the night.
Her husband thinks she's silly,

so the board is folded,
the money stacked by color,
and water runs in the bathroom
for a long time. But, in bed,

they pull each other close,
and why not?—each hauling
the other like found junk,
hoping to become something more

valuable, less bankrupt,
before the slow irony of dawn,
before the next cast of moon.
Together, in their yellow room,

they level their account:
a little motion that might pass
for travel, an overwhelming
desire to win without luck.

SINGLES

I don't know anyone more lonely
than the woman listening
to the late news, memorizing
baseball scores for coffee break.

She must undress so carefully,
folding her beige blouse
as if for the last time,
not wanting to be found unkempt

by detectives in the morning.
Sometimes I hear her talking
as she roams from room to room,
watering her plumeria,

the only splash of color.
She sets two places at the table
though no one ever comes,
then turns to the boredom of bed

thinking *Indians 7 – Yankees 3,*
Cardinals 11 – Mets 2
until she rises before dawn
and drives crosstown to work.

Could anyone be more lonely?
She doesn't acknowledge, again,
the man in the tollbooth
who's spent the whole night there,

not even a magazine before him,
grateful now to be making change
and touching fingers, briefly,
with such a beautiful stranger.

NEGATIVE SPACE

When you press next to me
on the downtown local, calm
in the clamor of secretaries,
the vast alarum of wheels,

toting your new sketchpad,
I imagine the flexed muscles
of the male model, the art
class you audit each night.

No one else notices you,
not even when the lights fail
and the train halts between stations,
when the air in the car grows stale

and, aloud, you begin to count
express trains flickering toward Queens.
Their lit windows bear faces
schoolchildren draw

in pencil on each fingernail,
though these faces are dimmer,
thinking of supper, thinking of bed,
the four hours of boredom between. . . .

The lesson this evening will be
to see what is *not* there,
to draw "negative space,"
the space, say, between two bodies,

say yours and mine, so palpable,
milky as the pulp
of the wet, green pears
ignored on the stool before you.

Their odor inhabits the air
so that, hours later,
entering your apartment,
the key still fixed in the lock,

you stare at the familiar furniture—
the sofa bed with its worn print,
the table with one leg
propped on newspaper,

the vase with its red, silk flower—
and see, not these still lifes, but
the terrible, torn spaces between them
you must, this moment, begin to fill.

BONWIT TELLER

Who says the light doesn't breathe
or press its thumbprint of snow
upon this rouged cheek
mirrored in the store window?

We stare—
            this reflection and I—
as she brushes her frosted hair
with her fingers, without regard
for little winds that tease the ends.

Above the roofs, the roof of snow
slowly collapses, but never touches
this landscape, so tropical,
where three mannequins,
                        almost nude
in the luminous, sand-strewn solitude,
    model bright bikinis—
stars wished above polished knees.

These familiar women also stare
into the fierce and artificial glare
of the yellow, foil sun—
while I pause among them, plump
ghost in a wet, woolen coat,
foolishly brushing my dampening hair.

Couldn't these sisters have prophesied
from their boiling cauldron of sun
what the future stores for flesh?—
how the various lights stress
each withering imperfection?

As a schoolgirl I stopped before this window,
closed my eyes, and rocked upon my flats
until the sidewalk seemed to undulate
and I grew dizzy with despair.
Will the change come? I sighed,
wanting to blossom into the sleek
skins, glossy thighs, impossible waists,
    bracelets and silver fox capes
that pronounced each flake of light.

Even their lashes were lovely, spidering
eyes opened forever in the stunned,
violet gaze of the paralyzed.
Will the change come soon?
Theirs was a perfect, breathless world.
The city could not touch them.

And I?—I stamp my galoshes for warmth,
embarrassed for the woman of snow
embarrassed now among them.
Their world remains, and remains
more eloquent than mine.

I realize the lateness of the hour, realize . . .
the buses will not run on time.

Only the glittering, gypsy taxis
like scarabs along the avenue,
the rows of traffic lights
shuttering—yellow,

     now red, now green—
a universe of diminishing suns,
and the million, heaving snowflakes
 light my skin
as if transforming me

     Will the change come?
into a speechless mannequin.

GREEN SHOES

Those green shoes on the curb
belong to the bum
sleeping in the doorway.
He wants the warmth of the sun

to inhabit them, to last
through another bitter night.
He'll doze until the traffic
grows heavy, businessmen

grinding home, then rise
to slip on those shoes—
still amazed by the perfect
fit, green shoes

thrown away by some big woman
no longer desiring to dance,
whose husband burst his heart
wrestling such strong legs.

He likes to imagine that!—
this bum who bears witness
each day among back alleys,
who tried them on, and grinned,

then tramped off as if owning
the whole blooming world,
still trusting dumb luck,
secure in the knowledge

the lost somehow find shelter,
the crippled always catch up,
the thirsty divine water,
the disinherited are welcomed

home wearing green shoes
polished with spit and sleeve,
green shoes flashing
fortune in the unblinking sunlight.

LUNCH HOUR

In the newspaper, another feature
  on the welder who fell six stories
    and lived, his impression

upon the blue roof of the Oldsmobile,
  his return, weeks later, to the site.
    Who expects such miracles these days?

Eating a ham sandwich, the mustard
  spicy on his tongue, he felt lucky:
    the city spread below him to the river,

the faded denim of sky,
  the sunlight celebrating anniversaries
    upon the rough architecture of his cheek.

Lunch hour, twenty minutes to the whistle,
  and nothing to do but gaze
    upon pigeons floating like paper,

the spires of downtown churches
  announcing their slender faiths.
    Last thing he remembered, he said,

was a shout, probably his own,
  that plunged with him like a bride,
    offering company unto the earth.

There's never a reason for loneliness,
  though it was created
    like this skyscraper, like pigeons

shitting among girders, the glittering cinders,
  eyeing some large, clumsy screech owl
    who's forgotten how to fly,

but flaps his arms anyway
  on this brief passage
    from one story to the next.

MORPHO

In his *Journey to the Jade Sea,*
"one of the world's greatest walkers," John Hillaby,
tells the story of the ebony child
raped and strangled
near an acacia tree in the bush in Kenya.
The game warden who found her was mesmerized
by two large, blue-green, rarely seen butterflies
trembling upon her glazed, staring eyes,
opening and closing their wings.
Those butterflies were attracted to moisture,
lapping with their spiked, black tongues
the shallow lagoons of primeval water.
Hillaby doesn't specify, but they were probably
    the *Morpho* butterfly,
each lulled in the mirror of her dissolving eye.
Beauty and beauty often go hand in hand—
"what an attractive couple," we say—
but some beauties are too terrible to bear.
I've only seen a dead woman once
outside of the Ridgewood Funeral Parlor.
In Amsterdam I wandered into a bar
where a three-hundred-pound, nude, quite dead woman
shaded the jungle of a back room pool table.
The club was hers, and she'd left provisions in her will
for the local populace to swill
the remaining stock in a sort of wake.
She was doused with beer
—the felt was soaked a deeper green—
and there, between her enormous thighs,

one silver-blue, scratchless, polished and buffed billiard ball
was blazing!
                    I was hypnotized.
I think that combination was beautiful,
or was near to what we think of as beauty.
Still, I couldn't look for long.
My duty was to accept another beer
and hoist it, in her dubious honor,
remembering, in another pocket of the world,
the mutilated girl with butterflies upon her.

"NIGHT IN THE TROPICS" (1858-59?)

> *"Lack of listeners did not deter Louis Moreau*
> *Gottschalk, living on the edge of a Guadeloupe volcano*
> *in 1859, from giving piano recitals to the universe."*
> —Edmund Morris
> "The Romance of the Piano"

Assuming *rain*, the exotic
species flare up like gas-flames
released from the earth, then settle on hibiscus
branches as the arpeggios shower down.
But the blossoms remain dry, their wings
dry, and only the spattering
notes keep them pinned to their trees, leaves
and insects blending in infinite
varieties.
      And the birds who pluck rare
butterflies from air, not finding them there,
assume *nightfall*, so return to their nests,
tongues stiff, though the sun slips
its staff of light through the canopies,
                  & so on
upward through the great chain of being, all
the bird-eating snakes, the snake-eating
birds, till the selection seems to halt,
Louis Moreau Gottschalk
slightly unnerved as he swabs the moisture
from the strings, shuts the lid of the Chickering,
then steps from the terrace into his room
to allow the universe to resume.

SNAKES

Knowing nothing about snakes, I fear them all—

the blunt, thumb-thick, foot-long diamondbacks
that idle in dry brush, motionless, for hours;

the sleek, sensual, black-eyed green snakes
that skate across the trail, then loop
around a vine, becoming the vine;

the flexuous, longer-than-I-am boa constrictors
that loll in swamp grass, gross,
rounded with a suckling
pig.

I have seen these snakes dead, hanging
full-length from a limb, being skinned
to be sold at the market in Limón.

I have seen them in my dreams, falling
from palm fronds, from rafters, from the sky.

Knowing nothing about snakes, I give them
their expanse, turn back on the narrow,
poorly-lit paths.

Ricardo, twice bitten, has given warning:
"A venomous snake will mate with a green. . .
what the guidebooks tell you is harmless
might kill you."
                          I turn away. I go back.

Knowing nothing about so many things,
I try to distinguish what's harmless
from what's not, who to be kind to,
where generosity lies.

But nothing should be ignored, nothing

doesn't matter, and even the common garter
sunning on a flat rock
can easily overwhelm us.

Costa Rica

SCORPIONS

How easy, lazy in this light-struck country,
   to grow familiar with the morning
      rituals: boil water from the well,

hang the empty egg basket on a nail
   for the frail farmer to fill,
      prop open shutters with rocks.

And rocks are more than abundant here
   where a man must shake his shoes
      like a nervous gambler at The Sands,

say, rattling his fist, then
   staring at what spills out—
      constellations of scorpions,

Rorschach blots come alive, the color
   of rancid butter, that yellow-going-to-brown,
      miniature skeletons awaiting flesh.

They click, broken dice, onto the stone
   floor, then scuttle into cracks
      before I bring the heel down.

Once I was stung on the thumb
   by a thimble-sized scorpion,
      and twice I've found two

locked together at the pincers,
   performing some arachnid mating
      magic or macabre toe-to-toe tango.

If you breathe on a scorpion,
   legend tells us, it burns bright blue,
      but whose lips would draw so close?

Yet who could consign even one
   to the lower concentrics of hell
      without regard to grand design?

Consider their power: to make a man
   meditate, ignore the sun
      to gaze into the shadows in his shoes.

Ios

TUNA

Icy with sea-surge, only three
　　green flies excavating
　　　　the vitreous humor
　　of its yellow eye, God-flung
galaxies perishing down the scales,
　　the tuna overhung the warped
　　　　wooden plank like Christ's
　　body, ribboned & bloody,
pried from the cross to be dressed
　　for its brief burial. But
　　　　must every fish in seven
　　oceans = Christian symbol?
Lemon leaves concealed the taverna
　　till the crone brandishing
　　　　her cleaver—*tono!*—
　　waved us beyond the trellis.
Then two seared slabs rinsed in oil.
　　Imagine how long the soul
　　　　must navigate the celestial
　　passages before its formal
dispersal, how long this creature
　　had tunneled the arctic
　　　　channels before delivering
　　its torn shoulder to our table,
before each flake of flesh
　　hesitated along the tongue,
　　　　then plunged the whole
　　body into blue-black mystery.

Crete

NAKED SEA BUTTERFLIES

Clione limacina

Like you, I don't know *what* they are,
having discovered the teasing,

seductive pleasure of their name
in some thumb-worn science journal

among *Peoples* spilling over
the doctor's waiting-room table,

but imagine them: translucent;
exhausted novae, fallen; black-

tipped pinwheels spinning upon vast
lattices of foam, each splintery,

pixel-like brain stem pulsing joy.
Who among us would compromise

any creature's brief happiness
with grief, however redemptive?

Like us, they may evolve without
sure knowledge of the exquisite,

without fame, even (unlike us)
without knowledge of the simple,

poetic dazzle of their name.

THE TURTLES OF SANTA ROSA

haul their leathery, pockmarked backs
across the ribbed, black marl

like locals rocked with bundles
of tourists' blue jeans and socks.

They deposit their spongy eggs
in pockets gouged in sand,

then turn—so slowly!—
like the hands of wound-down clocks

to rest before dragging
their plosive hearts beyond the breakers.

We prowl with flashlights
and kneel near the nests

to observe the annual ritual
of these hundred-year-old reptiles.

And what can these ancient
washerwomen think of us,

strange creatures generating light,
stepping among the carapaces

while murmuring softly
at the green, instinctual mystery?

Some nights we see their children
struggling from the sands.

Half-conscious, they eye us
on miniature, toy-like oars—

could *we* be their earthly mothers?—
before rowing their way unerringly

toward the ceaseless, nurturing
ululations of the waves.

So I dedicate these words
to the turtles of Santa Rosa

who, a century from now,
on the scrawled floor of the sea,

having grown gentle and enormous,
might then remember me.

Costa Rica

PASSION CONCH

No sun today, the rainy
   season barely begun, so
     we sleep late before

performing the instinctive,
   casual, tourists' ritual:
     combing the beach

in search of the unusual
   among the wrack and weedy
     debris. Ahead of me,

you scan the tide-
   line for what remains,
     the left behind, the false

and glittering sapphires
   the salt's slow churning
     has tossed ashore—

and pull up a shell
   still filled with muscle,
     purple with black

stitching, the heart's
   colors, pulsing:
     Passion Conch:

slug that has journeyed
  farther than we have,
    from silences deeper

than sleep, withstood
  pressure beyond weather,
    seining the forgotten,

prophetic psalms of the sea—
  all ear, or tongue,
    or one foot

probing, till arriving
  here, in your hand,
    object of our naming:

Passion Conch: tight knot
  of spongy knowledge,
    scholar of coral

passages, blind traveler
  absorbing the world:
    salt water, green

minutiae, perhaps two lovers
  biding time in the gray
    light, in light

rain, turning their deep
  desire over and over,
    having finally found,

in the foreign face,
   in the blunt, breathing
     body, a kindred

race, the source
   of flame, a gift,
     a name.

Hua Hin
Thailand

DRIFTWOOD

God's castoff sculpture on the lesser scale:
   forget the riven spines of mountain range or
      rubble-strewn calderas thrust above sea level.
Been there, done that, He might sigh. And Who
would compete with His own stubborn creation
   wasting a century to spire a single cathedral?
      So He works quickly, having read trendy
texts on the art of *not-thinking,* those Zen
tea salesmen who honor watchful ancestors
   by pouring ceremonial clouds of steeping
      leaves into tiny, ceramic cups, never
spilling a drop. One tear brims God's wide eye.
(Severe storm warnings flash along the coast.)
   He has no ancestors due homage, none
      to offer Him some thorny branch of wisdom.
So He allows His hands to begin their work,
oak after long-standing oak pared to a knobby
   stick, teeth-marked pencil, nubbed
      splinter, then begin again, till
the coaxed wood issues forth its primeval
soul, the cacophonous score of the creation
   captured in grooves and gnarls. This jazzy
      combo of wind and rain—God's callused palm,
His blunt right thumb—conjures now a tulle
fog beachcombers must part in order to touch
   what's been tossed along the littoral:
      these modest abrasions shape-shifting
   with sand fleas, this rank curvature,

the swirling grain's giddy abstractions
  beckoning the sidewise crabs who vex
    from one knotty installation to the next,
  stalk-eyed critics ragging this tidal
gallery of slathered grit, frothing *no Louise
Nevelson* while God sips one more scotch.
  Philistines, He fumes, *why do I bother?*
  but He won't return to marble, won't ever
go back to clay—why repeat Himself?
  He knows the artist has no choice
    but to bumble forward, abandoning
  each failure as He abandoned the grand
gesture, these crumbling continents, God's juvenilia.

GOD AT FORTY

I think God must be reading,
or crumpling love letters, or poking His cramped finger
into the ash of the dead
fire to resurrect the flames and warm His mildewed room.
Rain spatters the cabin roof.
One hushed breeze freshens the crab apple blossoms upstate
where God summers. They're pleasant,
these evenings spent in solitude, though God remembers
each of His former lovers
who steamed exotic meals for wary angels, Thai oil
to relieve the strict boredom
of living with a brooding Being whose creative pulse
drove Him inward, whose silence—
that dour guest—too often graced their bountiful table.
Now God keeps His meals simple,
noodle soup simmered on the single coil, peppered brie
slabbed on chunks of broken bread.
Late afternoons neighbors bring baskets of blueberries,
predict dry weather, then leave.
Near dusk God revises His poems, counting syllables—
traditional forms soothe Him
(though He prefers free verse), lend emotional restraint,
keep Him from stepping over
the border of sentimentality where minor
postmodernists stray. Not God.
His eyes water, the owl's clawed feet loose the poplar branch,
the fire wavers, and He sleeps.
Another shitty day in paradise, He might joke
on scrawled postcards never sent.
And dreams: unclasped bra, sunburnt back, freckled skin peeling.
Ants file the smoke-smudged ceiling.

One mouse scurries from its woodpile shelter, zigzags back.
Then God awakens, opens
His black binder to erase some easy metaphor.
He never answers prayers, but
heeds His morning routine: NPR, knee-bends, java,
then work, always the work, lost
for hours in rough drafts, until the broth boils, the cheese wedge
flicks its furred green tongue of mold,
or the last loaf crumbles, and God's immense loneliness
overwhelms. He scrapes His pocked,
bristly cheek along the splinter-shot table, eyes shut,
allowing His vast yearning
to wash over the planet, cool scouring blankness, that
leaf-lit, resplendent seepage
whose source He sometimes forgets—within Him or without?
Rain quickens the white dwarf pines.
God's manuscript blows open, thumbed leaves riffling, their chirr
the psalm of His rasped breathing.

PARADYS

"Of Paradys ne can not I speken propurly,
   ffor I was not there,"
      Sir John Mandeville joked in his *Travels*,

but in the six centuries of suffering
   since, the fortunate have been offered
      glimpses, rents in the archetypal

veil, fierce yet subtle glimmerings.
   I don't mean lovers, that sudden
      enlightenment as you're clasped

or kindled within, or museum-goers
   who envy Gauguin's Tahiti,
      or those minor poets who endlessly

exalt the vast stupor of childhood.
   No. I mean the multitudes
      who arrived by crutch

or bicycle or cart drawn by oxen
   or limb stunted since birth
      during the Festival of Lights—

who stooped to rest on the river
   frail boats of palm fronds,
      candles flaring silken cargoes

of lotus, then nudged them, gently,
   into the murmurous current
      till they caught and began

their spiraling descent, thousands of spirits
   conversant upon the waters
      in response to the beckoning stars.

Here, they seemed to answer,
   on earth where we belong. . . .
      Then we drifted anonymously

back to the abandoned city,
   a procession of feverish
      visionaries, until we dispersed

to our solitary travels, to grief,
   despair, the sickness of the age,
      Mandeville mapping his route

beyond the 14th Century, the sinuous
   journey toward a once-glimpsed
      but by-now-extinguished Paradys

still issuing forth, a continuum
   of the faithful, each pilgrim participant
      if ever we desire to enter.

                Chiang Mai
                Thailand

THE TORCHES

Limbs lopped off, the fathers
thrashed through the orchard
till a torch was touched to their hair
and they were consumed by the unearthly
love that lifted their souls toward heaven.
How impossible to mute the body with belief.
Women closed their shutters and crossed themselves.
Soldiers jeered. But the burning were beyond
the grievous clamor of the New World.

Clear sky that night, the thousand stars
assuming tentative shapes
like children assembling in the schoolyard.
Ashes smoldered on the hillside.
Then rain. By morning, only chipped dice and scorched soil remained.

What's irrefutable is that sweeping odor,
not the fume of charred tongues and gasoline,
but the first profuse blossoming of orchids,
a fragrant exhalation from the earth's core,
and those sudden shafts of light
crisscrossing in late afternoon
as the missing bear through the marketplace
their flaming tapers of spine, their wicks of hair.

Nicaragua

MILES WEEPING

To hear Miles weep
   for the first time, the notes bent
      back into his spent frame to keep
   them from soaring away—
I had to click the phonograph off
   and hug myself to stop the shaking.
      I'd recognized a human cry
   beyond any longing given a name.
If ever he let go that grief
   he might not touch his horn again.
      That cry rose in another country,
   full-throated in awkward English.
I still have the envelope, unstamped,
   addressed to "Mother / Father," its oily
      scrap of paper torn from a primer,
   the characters like the inky
root-hairs scrawling the washed-out soil.
   Lek—every boy's nickname—
      wrote he was "to be up against,"
   meaning, I guess, that his future
was end-stopped, one unbroken line
   of tabletops waiting to be wiped.
      He'd walked miles along the coast
   to find us combing the beach, then
stood, little Buddhist, with bowed head
   while we read his letter, composed
      with the help of the schoolmaster.
   How could we deny the yearning

ambition to abandon the impossible
   land of his fathers, to begin again?
      We could only refuse in a silent way.
   When someone asked Miles Davis
why he wouldn't play ballads anymore,
   he replied, "Because I love them too much."
      All that we never say to each other.
   The intimacies we can't complete.
Those ineluctable fragments. To be up against.

Koh Samui
Thailand

NOT JUST ANY DEATH

but the kind that comes to the lonely
like a reunion.
I don't want to see my friends.

Each night, deep inside you,
I feel myself moving even closer
to that certain loneliness

we must share with the dead.
I know that for each dozen times
I enter your body

I have entered another grave.
And with each six inches
there is another loneliness,

growing blacker,
like the corpse of the man
who entered death with anticipation.

RIVER WIFE

During lovemaking he fell asleep, one moment
mindless, churning like a propeller,
the next fallen away like a corpse tossed over
the lip of a scow into a spoiled estuary.
But he floated on the surface, less flesh than oil,
and my mind was more alert now
than when we'd returned from the church social.
Cool light rinsed the room.

                                    A sweet tongue—
the neighbor's who'd brushed past fox-trotters
to touch my arm, and I wished
I could have given myself to him wholly.
I was beginning to dream the trashy
novella, the intoxicating sin, the Ramada
on the bypass where the romance might begin,
the awkward undressing, then the minute
attentions to each yearning
ripeness of flesh

                        when the thumping began,
a distant sound that made me think
someone had entered the house and was stamping
booted feet. I almost woke
my husband by habit, but listened
to the dull reports—gunshots?—, then rose
to creep by ear to the summer porch,
then out into the yard toward the shed.
Frost stippled my skin
and the moon gazed frankly upon my nakedness.
The booming beckoned
though the shed door was bolted shut.
Rasping its hinge, I poked past shovels and rusted traps

to hear the thumping stop, then start.
A rubber barrel thundered each burst
and inching near I glimpsed the rat, larger
than a rat, nightmare of teeth and hair, berserk
with thirst and singular intent, leaping again and again
against the curved walls toward the impossible hatch.
I clamped the barrel with its lid, repulsion
rattling my ribs, secured the latch,
then hefted it to the barn,
the rat shifting but quiet now within.
I thrust the barrel into a stall.
But back in bed I couldn't sleep
as the furious thrashing resumed, someone
pounding a hammer across the river, someone
unable to stop the current threatening to sweep away her house.
I don't know when I fell asleep,
but by first light the noise had ceased.
I tramped to the barn through mist and slapping reeds
and removed the lid to find—
                    nothing.
The barrel was empty. The rat
had eaten through the rubber and slipped into the river.
That dawn I let what sun there was
strike me on the breast, absorbed the flame,
then turned to stare down the stagnant house
growing paler in the glimmer reflected off the river.

THE FOX

After we peeled and dipped and sucked
each leaf of the artichoke
to reveal the fluted
heart still steaming in its shaggy
rind, after uncorking another light-proof
bottle of homemade plum wine, we began
telling our dreams, those that surprise us
or bring back the romantic
childhood urgencies long ago given over
to the conservative wishes of adults—
the wish to be simple, to hurt no one—
when, low to the earth, scavenging the frost-
lit bristles of saw grass for torpid mice,
the fox appeared beyond the glass door,
tarnished silver, mottled with mange,
a rough rag torn from the hillside,
a storybook fox cut out with blunt scissors.
The retrievers shook off their sleep then,
ramming shoulders against the door,
slathering the thick panes with foam
till we hauled them, choke-chain, back.
The fox paused, gazing at the hushed
gathering only heartbeats away, then sidled off
into the muffled trees, leaving us
astounded, more than pleased, aware
of a mild blessing bestowed upon friends.
Later that night, I glimpsed our host's face
pressed to the guest-room window
while my wife and I undressed. Startled,
I yelled, and he quickly stalked away
among wavering stems of starlight.

During the awkward breakfast, he mentioned
how he'd gone out in search of the fox,
but found nothing but scat,
the autumn earth too hard for tracks.

Sometimes I dream of the fox in his lair,
that secret, interior life
growing thinner, losing hair, starving,
the alert intelligence sharpened by need
helpless not to transform itself into grief,
humiliation, the tense silence among friends
in return for a moment of mournful
revelation, the chimera of a child,
however naked and heart-rending, however
impotent and wild.

DOGS IN THE STORM

after Akhmatova

When this slow heart was raging
and I could tell no one, especially you,
I would abandon the exhaustion of sheets,
this woman tossing like damp leaves,

and storm a few miles into the country.
I wanted to memorize the silhouette
of each branch, the chorus of stars,
the uproar of the willows' shadows,

the stiff mailboxes bearing witness
to such immense drift and flux.
I wanted not to think about you.
But each time some stray bitch

came limping along the highway,
eyes iced shut in wind, nose
scenting the hunger of wild couplings,
I wondered: Whose lost lover is this?

And how far away is my distant brother
who howls for us both in such savage moonlight?

VILLAGE DOGS

1990

Groggy, we watched the ball descend
    as benediction upon the boisterous
        throng overflowing Times Square.
            We felt no desire

to mill there, to embrace the New
    Year among strangers, jostled and cold.
        Corks still popping at nearby
            parties, I leashed the dog only

minutes past midnight and let him lead me
    onto the village street, its one lamp
        a low moon lustrous below black
            clouds, glazed with rain.

What remained unspoken between us followed me
    like a shadow in a B movie, then sprang
        through a hedge wall with a primal
            snarl. A pit bull, frothing

knot of muscle, slammed into my pet like a small
    train, tumbling him, his high-pitched
        yelps rising above their revved
            thrashings and the revelers' shouts.

I kicked and missed and thudded onto my back
    inches from their slathered, blood-
        slick snouts. *Match days of sorrow,*
            decrees Psalm 90, *with days of joy . . .*

I rose and dragged my broken dog
  by the choke-chain toward the house,
    the bull still clamped to his throat
      till I splintered a branch across its spine.

By now my wife stood pale on the porch
  as I hefted a brick to crush
    its skull, but her cry stopped my arm:
      "Don't. Haven't you done enough harm?"

The bull foamed in the hedge's shadow.
  I hurled the brick into its ribs
    and the creature—my stunted anger—
      fled with a groan. And when I returned

home, bruised and sober, the neighbors'
  festive clamor dwindling
    in the decade's first hour, who
      could deny that the marriage was over?

GREEN ASH, RED MAPLE, BLACK GUM

How often the names of trees consoled me,
how I would repeat to myself *green ash*
while the marriage smoldered in the not-talking,
red maple when the less-than-tenderness flashed,
then *black gum, black gum* as I lay next to you
in the not-sleeping, in the not-lovemaking.

Those days I tramped the morass of the preserve,
ancient ash smudging shadows on stagnant pools,
the few wintry souls skulking abandoned wharves.
In my notebook I copied plaques
screwed to bark, sketching the trunks' scission,
a minor Audubon bearing loneliness like a rucksack.

And did the trees assume a deeper silence?
Did their gravity and burl and centuries-old patience
dignify this country, our sorrow?

So as I lay there, the roof bursting with invisible
branches, the darkness doubling in their shade,
the accusations turning truths in the not-loving,
green ash, red maple, black gum, I prayed,
in the never-been-faithful, in the don't-touch-me,
in the can't-bear-it-any-longer,
black gum, black gum, black gum.

TWO BATHS

One

Lovelier than Susannah
who set the elders' hearts groaning at twice their faithful
stride, so that each grandfather
clutched his breast to remember the beauty of the nude
female body, you tilted
the pail to plash well water over stepped terraces
of flame-red hair, rivulets
snaking down breasts, God-thumbed birth-stain, vulval thatch and thighs.
And I lavished the shampoo
as you knelt in the rue anemone, spiraea's
windfall stippling burnished skin,
lather foaming through my fingers, foaming shut your eyes
as you took me in your mouth,
the sun bearing witness to our blind, intuitive
coupling, till I tipped the pail
to rinse our fallen flesh, let our imperfections glisten.

Two

Light roused us from the depths of our separate longings
and while I balanced buckets
you laced black sneakers for your morning run on the cliff,
wrapped the red ribbon of shirt
around your forehead, stretched stiff calf muscles, then ran off.
I could see you jog the beach
as I arranged notebooks, pens, on the marble table,
then begin the zigzagging
goat path toward the crag overlooking our stone cottage,
your red rag still visible
against the rough, anemic marble of the mountain.
Remember the undressing,
how I slipped off your Nikes, peeled each slick of cotton,
then unknotted the sweatband
and dipped that tatter into the icy water, sponge
pressed between your breasts, your legs,
the tenderness between us before the sex turned sour?—
before your six miles became
a more-than-tacit withdrawal, like sleep, or headphoned jazz,
so I'd watch you crest the hill
as I worked at the marble table, wrenching lines, syl-
lables, the diminishing
sweatband a raw wound in the distance, as I revised
draft after draft, prodding you
past the horizon, writing you out of existence.

Ios

PARTHENOPI

Once we beheld the brilliance of our estate
reflected in the haloed serenity of the girl
who prepared the basketful of cucumbers for salad,
slicing each nub into watery wheels,
columns of coins in the egg-white bowl.
Then she'd lift each miniature transparency
as she'd seen the priest flourish the Host,
thumb the serrated blade
to nick the green, then twist her wrist
to peel back the dust-plumed skin, the rubbery shavings
heaping a wild garden, unspoiled Eden, on the wooden counter.
Again and again she consecrated each wafer.
We basked in her patience, that rapt transportation,
her bell-shaped, narrowing eyelids as she spun
one papery sun, then the next, her perfect happiness,
smoke from the blackened grillwork wreathing her hair,
the fat of the slaughtered lamb hissing in the fire.
Her name—we'd asked our waiter—was Parthenopi, "little virgin."
We were still a couple then, our summer's lazy
task to gather anecdotes toward one future,
each shared and touching particular
to be recited over baked brie and chilled chardonnay
in the grasp of some furious, if distant, winter.
"Parthenopi," one of us might say, chiming a glass,
but the common measure of love is loss.
The cucumbers glistened in oil and thyme.

Ios

HUMMINGBIRDS

When I read the translation from the Russian,
razdirat' dushu, literally, to "tear out" one's soul,
I understood the genesis of hummingbirds,
how they can be there and not-there,
how the specific wind of their wings
trembles the three leaves of the sassafras,
how the tumescent tongues of the lilies clamor their presence.

How the elements conspire to create them:
the blue-green pearl of molten sand
—that miniature globe, swirl of smoke—
hovering at the tip of the glassblower's rod
seems forever on the verge of cooling
into final form, the almost-shape of the hummingbird.

At the dinner party, no longer lovers,
we spoke to each other in such measured tones
to keep our voices from modulating,
until you couldn't help but choose
not to return my gaze, or respond to my mild jokes.
I felt some interior wall tumble away. . . .

Who has ever seen a hummingbird arrive?

Who has seen a hummingbird at ease, though
its metaphysical dollop of flesh
must grow heavy, weighted with gravity, even
the saffron seed of its eye, the cork skeleton,
the heart like a ball bearing in its feathered case.

What I've never told you is that, beyond the ruins,
I glimpsed a garden
resplendent with hummingbirds,
an aviary of exiled souls
working so hard just to remain in one spot.

SHHH

The language that remains unspoken, often
for years, till the shuddering rhythm of the Accord

helps to shape a stanza you revise aloud
in splendid isolation, becomes another version of *goodbye*

still less eloquent than Miles' muted "Shhh" on FM
& arriving much too late to make leaving easier for either.

"If I love you," wrote Goethe, "what business is it of yours?"
So the spondees that propel your dented shell this evening

begin to dissipate in the never-imagined future-without-her
like gasoline fumes floating from your fingers,

while those smoky solos—how she clasped you within her!—
resonate like the muffled clamor of orgasm, chords

blown beyond improvisation, beyond prosody, till
you surrender destination, your stress-laden vocabulary,

to the tires' susurration on the sodden leaves, & the slow,
unbroken seeping-upward of the combo. *Shhh.*

THE BURDEN LIFTERS

At least you left me the green
   dial of the radio
      sending forth its watery

light as I listened
   to the all-night talk
      shows till, bored with G

spots, vigilantes, the midnight
   madness at Crazy Eddie's,
      I tuned in the gospel

station, letting Willis Pittman
   and his Burden Lifters
      undo the damage of too

much talk—their harmonies
   soared above New York,
      held back the endless

babble of traffic, reduced
   the hubbub of static
      to a hush. In the back-

ground rose the sound
   of women weeping, trudging
      to the altar to be touched

by some euphoric preacher
   for the sake of the souls
      of their junk-ridden sons.

How many phone calls did I make,
  prayer aprons purchase
    from Reverend Ike, a host

of DJs spanning the seaboard,
  wanting someone to bless
    the hurt away, lift

my burden, let me groan,
  Lord, into the black
    telephone till dawn

eased down its light,
  gentle fingers upon
    my godforsaken shoulders?

SIMPLE HAPPINESS

You have done too much of the exquisite,
Henry James consoled Whistler, *not to have earned*
more despair than anything else.
You have sponged the storm windows
and raised them, then lowered summer's screens
to allow the feathery brume of pollen
to sweep into your room. And you have stepped,
barefoot, across the muffled wooden slats,
trailing footprints from the bed to the shower
where you smoothed the green oval of soap
over your arms and breasts and belly,
let the sulfurous waters jet
the pollen from your hair till the foam
swirling into the basin burst
bright yellow. And you have shaken open the towel
from the wicker basket to buff your coral
body dry, then sprinkled powder onto one palm,
small puffs burgeoning the swollen layers of air.
I sit at my table imagining your morning,
the pollen that pummeled your flesh
tumbling room to room till blown across rooftops
to sift down into soft heaps around me, infinitesimal
stars signaling the explosion of one galaxy
and the slow, laborious creation of the next,
and by now you have pressed your face
into the faded flowers of your dress,
remembering that passage I read to you,
Svevo in a letter to his beloved Livia:
. . . to hear that you had wept
gave me hours of simple happiness.

NEW HOPE

The unforeseeable future, your absence assuming
    texture, arrives this October dusk
against the glass doors with such force, rainwater
    striking revisions upon the panes,
that the blown landscape, half-acre of ragged
    grasses, wavers & blurs, the evergreens
showering their thousand, combustible needles
    across the rotted planks of the deck.
Tomorrow I'll sweep away these clumped splinters
    to find among sap-clotted cones & papery
wasps' nests the scattered shards of the red
    & yellow hummingbird feeder, fiery
puzzle, each gaudy fragment the shape of a state
    we drove through, inch by mile,
to imagine our lives bound beyond the country
    inns & heaped breakfast trays,
beyond the exhaustion of AAA maps.
    This was your gift, not the beckoning
feeder or ceaseless, brassy chimes, but the quick
    dissolution of our plotted landscapes
for the sake of a central clarity: you & I
    in a pencil-post bed in some eighteenth-
century manor overlooking the Delaware River,
    trapped in the irony, one trip, of a town
named New Hope, the feeder unwrapped & dangling
    from the mirror, doubled brilliance
among crumpled newspaper wads. That last weekend
    a sudden squall funneled down the Gap,
alarming the Sunday boaters, couples racing
    both banks back to musty rooms, the far

shore barely visible from our balcony, but
  someone still there, perhaps a child,
calling, over & over, in a dying caterwaul
  muffled by foam, what sounded like your name.

AVESTA

God's sparrow blown from its branch in the storm
splits open upon the mole-riddled lawn.
Her nest still tumbles among the yellow
horsemint and false nettle. Her nestlings lie
broken, transparent. Zoroastrians
take solace in a multiplicity
of souls, leaving cadavers exposed but
fettered so that no bone might be scattered,
missing on the day of resurrection.
Here in suburbia I let these birds
loose their odor of rot beyond the oak.
But I scoop up their nest, almost weightless,
to find—months after you've gone—coppery hairs
tendriling twigs and scraps of yarn, uncial,
some woven fragment of the sacred text:
Ahura Mazda requiring good deeds
to aid in his struggle against evil.
Light combs through the residual moisture,
illuminating souls that inhabit
ciphers of feather, eggshell, scavenged lock.
You'd prowled the deck that solstice dawn, naked
except for slashed panty hose, allowing
our neighbors, stunned over coffee, to stare
as you savaged your incandescent hair,
scissors crazed like some Hitchcockian flock.
The nest crumbles now into filaments
encircling my hand, your footfall almost
audible in each shorn, familiar strand.

B&B

Let's begin here: three years later
we meet in a B&B only days after
the boy disappears in a lake in a distant state,
then's found, drowned & bitten, shredded torso
nosed through reeds by a 12-foot gator.
I read the local paper while you unpack, hanging
each whispery sheath like a ghost in the closet,
tucking unmentionables in the nightstand drawer.
His mother sets the picnic table: plastic forks,
paper plates, mustard & ketchup in squeezable bottles.
Cans of soda on ice in the cooler.
One sister's old enough to start the fire,
stacking a pyramid of black briquets.
Already the room grows humid with strangers.
The boy wades knee-deep, toeing green muck,
vertical piglet zeroed through a third eyelid.
Spooning salad, his mother swivels.
Gone. Wild incomprehension. Then worse.

Three years ago: we can't bear it any longer.
A boy named Jeffrey is born in Florida
to be torn open on a singular afternoon
as a thin spray of fluid douses charcoal
& one struck match arcs into the grill. *Whoosh*.

RUBY-THROATED HUMMINGBIRD

Archilochus colubris

. . . *the red he uses has an astonishing vibration,*
    Gauguin envied Cézanne in his journal,
but red can shut the eyes, evoking war,
    the casual erasure of populations.
I prefer green, the shade you sometimes see
    on hummingbirds, those iridescent
compensations, though even John James Audubon
    couldn't get them quite right—I mean
their *presence*, their magisterial splendor,
    their monarchies among the honeysuckle . . .
how the adult male ruby-throated hummingbird
    fuses Cézanne's red vibration
with Gauguin's artless, pacific green,
    a commingling that lovers sometimes fulfill,
blending themselves till they can no longer tell
    from whose body the whirring begins.

THE INARTICULATE

Touching your face, I am like a boy
who bags groceries, mindless on Saturday,
jumbling cans of wax beans and condensed milk

among frozen meats, the ribboned beef
and chops like maps of continental drift,
extremes of weather and hemisphere,

egg carton perched like a Napoleonic hat,
till he touches something awakened by water,
a soothing skin, eggplant or melon or cool snow pea,

and he pauses, turning it in his hand,
this announcement of color, *purple* or *green*,
the raucous rills of the aisles overflowing,

and by now the shopper is staring
when the check-out lady turns and says,
"Jimmy, is anything the matter?"

Touching your face, I am like that boy
brought back to his body, steeped
in the moment, fulfilled but unable to speak.

THE FAITHFUL

Sometimes, when the world
no longer seems capable of surprise,
when your wife rehearses
the usual gestures of affection

and birches offer their annual
assortment of autumn leaves,
you forget how small the heart
might be, how fragile.

One morning, rushing to work,
you brush past a stranger
more beautiful than the dark
bruise of adolescence—

your fingers tracing a breast
at fourteen, your tongue
blooming with the moisture
on your sweetheart's throat—

and the world fashions a frail
shell, a pale rind,
the air within billowing
with the scent of buds unfolding,

so that in the story
you'll tell tonight to your children,
the cobbler in a barren country
lets fall his apron

to find not nails but
breathing, miraculous roses.

COGNAC

> Sometimes I sing so pretty
> I like to break my own heart.
> —Jimmy Durante

Each summer I would coddle a bottle of cognac
like a birth-blind calico,
then wedge it behind the cabinet's highball glasses
rather than among the stumped
veterans of mash, clear church bells of Finnish vodkas
and swan-necked, elegant slips
of sage and flame liqueurs, so that, reunion over,
we might retrieve it alone,
the two of us, and sip blunt amber that sandpapered
our throats into intimate
speech. We slumped, string-snipped marionettes, onto chintzy
cushions, heads humped together,
to resume dissection of longtime spouses, elsewhere
asleep despite suspicions,
our feral children, and the longing glimpsed in simple
gestures of close friends even
as they'd sponged glasses or rearranged half-drained bottles.
Our bottle squatted, muffled
telephone, genie-less lamp, allowing dialogue
its course—our voices bearing
their sad, sexual embassies, their torqued pleasures, their
"mystic current of meaning."
Each summer our too-brief encounter—solstice weekend—
distilled itself into mulled
smoke, brassy phosphor, cognac we prodded toward dawn till
the stories had been consumed,
their light absorbed in slow, deliberate sips toward depths

cross-channeling forever-
foreign flesh, our bodies drifting inexorably
toward final rigidity
as we'd kiss, almost chaste, then sleep, tongues swollen with false
fire, annual ritual,
cognac seeping into dreams, into the bearable
future still flush with desire.

SINCE NOTHING IS IMPOSSIBLE

This is a simple poem
because our lives can be simple. On the pier,
listening to the fish
gather in the shallow waters, the wind
blowing across the phosphorus,
I stood for hours in the pale halos of the harbor.

I was thinking of you, the way
an arm remembers salt burning the skin. Slowly,
with desire, I swept
one arm across the waters until its shadow,
like a black angel,
touched a school of minnows, parting them . . .

nothing more than a shadow, but
those minnows were forever brushed with wings,
the beating of one moment, the immense
blackness. So now
it has become this simple:
I want to enter you with nothing.

FIRST LESSON: WINTER TREES

These winter trees charcoaled against bare sky,
   a few quick strokes on the papery
      blankness, mean to suggest the mind
   leaping into paper, into sky, not bound
by the body's strict borders. The correspondence
   school instructor writes: *The ancient*
      masters loved to brush the trees
   in autumn, their blossoms fallen.
I've never desired the trees' generous
   flowering, but prefer this austere
      beauty, the few branches nodding
   like . . . like hair swept over a sleeping
lover's mouth, I almost thought too fast.
   Soon enough these patient alders
      will begin to blossom in their wild
   unremembering to inhabit the jade,
celebratory personae of late summer.
   So the task is simple: to live
      without yearning, to kindle
   this empty acre with trees touched
by winter, to shade them without simile,
   without strain. There: the winter trees.
      Their singular, hushed sufficiency.
   Again. Again. Again. Again. Again.
Now you may begin to sketch the ceaseless winter rain.

FIRST MILE

Not much of a challenge to anyone
    who'd spent winter tripling laps at the Y,
        but crossing Lake Forgotten dock to dam
    seemed an apt test at the time, so we dove,
then spoke as we eased past fanned pads, in shade,
    stroking the lake's slithery underskin.
        Our talk turned intimate— your arms flashing
    above that mirror, braceleted with weed,
beckoned me as I slowed in your wake,
    spuming *uh-huh* in response to my name.
        At the dam we hauled ourselves up
    onto the stone ledge to rest, brushing
hands and thighs, and the promise unspoken
    in any green romance dazzled in spindrift
        shaken from your hair. Who
    wouldn't be stunned, balanced on that lip
between the pent-up seepage and nowhere,
    the drop-off to the umbrage
        steep, leaving us no choice
    as we sidled off moss
to begin the slippery mile back.
    But I grew weak, our cadence ceased
        as you surged ahead in your own fatigue
    till you lay toweled on the dock
watching me crawl the lake, dog-paddling,
    floating now on my back, anything
        to worry me closer to the ladder.

SNOW CONE

Her tongue mimicked the color of her bikini
   after she'd licked the cherry
     snow cone, & the tip of the paper cup
    dripped fluorescent beads of syrup,
cool pinpricks, onto her oiled belly,
   the electric swirl pooling her pierced
    navel where the gold ring flashed.
  I told her its glittering would attract
sharks, how a novice scuba diver
   skimming the reef off the Caribbean
    coast of Costa Rica—I smiled at her—
had been taken headfirst into the maw
of a six-foot mako & blamed the attack
   on the cluster of studs rimming one ear.
    He'd managed to tear free & flail wildly
  to shore. Here I stroked her plaited hair.
The scars raking his skull seemed tribal,
   hewn in some Land-That-Time-Forgot coming-of-age
    ritual, but the raw stubs of his lobes
  oozed a milky gel that caked his cheeks.
As she jerked her braised shoulders
   in a tableau of revulsion, undone
    straps whisking sand, the icy
  flavor overflowed her belly button,
ruby rill snaking toward her tan-line,
   then under the rim of triangular cloth.
    She gazed at me now, propped on both
  elbows, the snow cone like a splintery bulb
generated by body heat, its slow leak
   shape-shifting her pubis into a relief
    map of a savvy Third World country
  that exports slashed fins for soup

but saves, for the occasional tourist
   blundering through the market square
     in search of a cheap souvenir,
   the sun-bleached, primeval hoops of teeth.

SEMEN

Seminis emissio est partes anima jactura.

Who remembers now in our millennial loneliness
  how some wise women during the '70s
    withheld one article of clothing—
  flimsy chemise or ribbed thigh-high—
to retain a semblance of control even
  while coming, not wanting to abandon
    themselves wholly?—though my Sunday
  lover, the jazzercise instructor,
lived in an efficiency rented by a married
  CEO who visited only once or twice
    each week. On one wall, the familiar
  photo of Nijinsky; on another, herself,
gifted student, almost nude, the crimped
  fringes of the fan-blown scarf
    barely trailing the studio slats. . . .
  Some couples still keep that singular
distance, each from each, a sacred
  grove; so Aulus Celsus, Roman
    encyclopedist, understood
  that "the ejaculation of semen
is the casting away of part of the soul"—
  but *not* how that holy fragment
    sparks a fire in a seaside cave,
  beckoning other whispery
tissues of the imperishable . . .
  leading, at last, to some dismal
    February when your wife, riding
the subway, feels suddenly suffused

with uncommon desire that she'll breathe
 back into your throat that night
  once you shuttle home from work.
 But that dancer, the disco era . . .
I remember repeating to myself:
 I am not her lover. I am not her lover.
  Only Nijinsky can be her lover,
 Nijinsky who remains mad, and dead.

NOT LOVE

Summer dusks, sunglare planing the back
   door, off-white paint curling
into flakes, fine ash, the wood weather-
   worn and almost hieroglyphic, I lift
the potted plant, night-blooming cereus
   flown east by a lover now distant,
and prop it on the warm stone steps
   so the sheaths might ease
upward and each leaf bathe in deepening
   glow. And grow. I tilt
water brimming the lip of a coffee can
   onto loose, black soil, then spoon
what pools from the saucer. Such tender-
   ness for these green yearnings,
slips whose only desire seems to be
   to awaken into final simplicity.
Urge and urge and urge, yawped Whitman.
   I want to awaken when the cereus
flowers to clip one cold blossom
   before it fails and press it between
ragged leaves of the 1892 "Death-Bed" edition
   for that woman I couldn't love
long enough, and for whom, not loving,
   I began to perfect these small,
sacramental gestures so that whatever tendril
   flourished between us might still
thrive, and her gift, however fragile,
   transmuted from the physical
world to the rough language of the text,
   might, after death, survive.

IF I DIE

If I die, I would like to come back.
Those trees planted in the garden
might be grown, blooming.
Nothing dead

would inhabit their bright plot.
I would come back to taste
the apples hanging from a black
branch, each one

small, round, almost perfect,
a bag of blood,
a bullet-hole in the air,
the wound already closing.

If I could, I would come back
to the house settling on the marsh,
the slow curve of the hill
rising, now, like heaven.

I would place my gray lips
on the cold pane,
on the silhouette of a woman
who stops, alert, listening . . .

and I would lie down, again,
in this familiar portion of earth,
a guest among the trees,
and dream each night of coming back . . .

DIVINE WILL

for M. in Romania

Seven hours: late afternoon here, lightning
　　stuttering the clocks, the stunned
　　　air a bronze bell one tick
　　past tolling—but already midnight
at the café where you're sipping vodka
　　with your former lover who's grown
　　　impatient with abundance:
　　the foil-wrapped chocolates, icy heaps
of scallops, thousand cereals, & Borgesian
　　library of toilet papers, blue & yellow,
　　　beyond wobbly pyramids of avocado
　　fluorescing the supermarket where we shop.
You've mentioned me only once, though
　　smoke-plumes loitering near the stuck
　　　ceiling fan assume foreplay in his gaze,
　　so he smudges one last cigarette onto the tabletop.
Seven hours: despite this sporadic flickering,
　　I'm still reading—the unsurprisingly
　　　brief biography of Luisa Piccareta,
　　Little Daughter of the Divine Will
b. Corato, Italy 1882 d. Corato, Italy 1947
　　who survived on nothing but Communion
　　　wafers for sixty-five years.
　　"She lived in her bed, and died each day.
Each day, in order for her to return to life,
　　a priest had to come—usually
　　　one of her five confessors—
　　to give her the order to obey him

and return to life." The lamplight fails,
   then flares. Hummingbird feeders
     twist among black branches,
   then dangle like gaudy fishhooks.
Your sullen ex watches as you slip
   two dollars under the empty
     ashtray, then crumple them back,
   embarrassed by your mistake, before
fingering the still-familiar lei.
   We tender ourselves to a will
     less divine, hurly-burly,
   here & there, floats & solutions.
Seven hours: soon you'll fly west, erasing
   the difference, cradling in your skirt
     six hollow eggs, airy gifts,
   hand-painted for the Orthodox Easter.

BOUNTIFUL

Providence leads us to many tables
in our travels, to meetings with the insignificant
others who, placing olives on their tongues,
begin to shine like the swollen Buddha.

Watching them eat, we fill with desire.
The raw broccoli in its cradle of ice
quivers its antennae, breathing its green
and vinegary aroma into the room.

Lemons offer their soft, underwater light.
Pale crescents of peaches in Bordeaux,
cheeses defining the shaded meanings of *yellow*,
chunks of melon like the fabled jewels of pharaohs,

the breast of turkey whiter than the linen
wrapping the risen body of Jesus—
you know the kind of meal I mean.
When the bread is broken, love seems possible.

If the sleep that follows draws us away
from this life into another, more abstract landscape,
food eases us into a future
among friends, among the forbearing women.

And sorrow has no place at this table,
simmering in black pots on back burners,
or remaining in cookbooks
bought by husbands roaming malls after the divorce.

ROMANCE IN THE OLD FOLKS' HOME

First he offered to read to her,
but she was afraid
he spoke as Bible-thumper, so declined.

Then he steeped several
herbal teas for her table—
she sipped without looking up.

He scissored photos from weeklies
and taped them to her door,
little windows into the past:

couples skating on Highland Pond,
dancing four days in a marathon,
sleeping on roofs above Flatbush Avenue.

She knew she was being spoken to
in a language long forgotten,
like Latin lost after school.

When she found the horned shell
near her lounge on the lawn,
she pressed it to her ear

to hear the ceaseless *hush*,
knowing longing had replaced
the sluggish creature housed there.

The next evening she appeared
with freshly washed hair
pinned with an ivory comb,

and brought that shy spirit
her favorite book—
The Marble Faun by Nathaniel Hawthorne

who liked to brood on sin—
while the faint widows flushed
and whispered her name—oh Anna!—

and she asked him please to begin.

KEATS' LIPS

1

In the death mask by Gherardi,
the flesh has already fled
the formal bones of the face,
    chiseled cheek and belled brow,

but the lips remain swollen,
almost pursed, what's left
of Keats' tumultuous spirit
    struggling to forsake the mouth.

Keats might have been his own
best poem, transmutable as smoke,
but his lips were impassable:
    "I lifted him up in my arms,"

Severn wrote, "and the phlegm
seemed boiling in his throat."
And when the body was no more
    than a flask, the last vial

of blood broken in his lungs,
the sticks of foreign furniture,
encrusted linens and nightshirt,
    even the door and window frame

were taken by the police
and set aflame in the piazza
below the barren, February steps,
    Bernini's marble boat

showering the air, bearing
the antique smell of Keats'
earthly possessions toward the sea
in the slow swirl of its grain.

2

His death mask lies in glass,
facing a sky the color of straw.
The fireplace in his room is shut.
Tourists throng the square

when the steep steps flower
and the light veers violet,
sift maps in Babington's Tea Room
and loiter below Keats' window.

In the hotel that night we argued,
hurt each other with words,
then made love, that blind, desperate
lovemaking born of loneliness.

Let me tell you this—
when our faces flushed with orgasm,
as we briefly lost all control,
I was praying for Keats, his lips,

the language touched with fever
that bears us away from our bodies
and soothes the bruised soul,
if only for a few moments.

We rose with the clamor
of street cleaners and vendors
fronting fruit stands and flower stalls
to find the sun still cloaked

with smoke rising off the Tiber.
Keats loved the light on his face
when he paused on the promenade,
and gathered momentary faith

when the hundred gray pigeons
began their awkward, flapping ascent
toward the gables and red tiles,
then vanished above the rooftops.

CREATION

Vollard loved to tell his clients this story—

Degas, having arrived late for dinner,
paused with his host in the hushed, crowded parlor
—this host was a famous Parisian collector—
to view his painting recently hung there:
young ballerinas after rehearsal, sprawling backstage
or pivoted at the waist to untangle satin laces,
their hair cascading palest pinks and yellows,
exuding a weary, unself-conscious beauty.
Degas stared and stared till, without a word,
he lifted the picture in its gilt-edged frame
from its spot on the wall, the guests aghast,
then hefted it home under his arm
that he might retouch one dancer's limb.
He never returned the painting, never
passed near that gentleman's house again
while—here Vollard would clap his hands!—
all over Montmartre patrons of the arts
chained their Degas to their parlor walls.

Who hasn't been taught that a work of art
is never finished, but always "abandoned"?
Some tinker forever, souls fluttering in wrists,
allowing the light to surrender each stroke.

Imagine God's exhaustion once the earth
neared completion, before man was abandoned
to video arcades and two-story malls. . .
His infinite elation, the week's work gone well,
how He even transcended His own limitations—

then that inconsolable letdown, the probable certainty
that He could never again populate a planet
even if He took all of eternity, never again
bear to face such a vast, virginal
burnished white waste and,
beyond this, *how*

              —the planet spinning now, luminous
as the archetypal pearl—
did He ever manage to float such a world?

ACKNOWLEDGMENTS

Not Just Any Death. BOA Editions. 1979.
Green Ash, Red Maple, Black Gum. BOA Editions. 1997.

I remain grateful to the late A. Poulin, Jr. of BOA Editions for his encouragement and support.

Grateful acknowledgment is made to Carnegie Mellon University Press for permission to reprint poems from the following books:

Anniversary of the Air (1985): "The Mystery of the Caves," "American Bandstand," "Mythology," "Singles," "The Faithful," "Monopoly," "Dogs in the Storm," "Negative Space," "Bonwit Teller," "Lunch Hour," "Green Shoes," "Anniversary of the Air," "Pollen," "The Story of the Caul";

The Burden Lifters (1989): "Horse," "Reading Dickens," "Lipstick," "Brooklyn Waterfall," "The Conversion of Saint Paul," "Foundling," "Burning the Dolls," "Snakes," "Keats' Lips," "Yellow Stars," "The Burden Lifters," "Morpho," "The Turtles of Santa Rosa," "Passion Conch," "Romance in the Old Folks Home";

Bountiful (1992): "Creation," "'Night in the Tropics' (1858–59?)," "Homo Sapiens," "Covert Street," "Singing for Elizabeth," "Shadow Boxes," "The Difference Between a Rooster and a Whore," "Scotch and Sun," "Bountiful," "Shhh," "The Inarticulate," "Hummingbirds," "The Fox," "River Wife," "Village Dogs," "The Torches," "Paradys," "Miles Weeping," "Scorpions."

Grateful acknowledgment is made to the editors of journals in which these poems, often in earlier versions, first appeared:

The American Poetry Review; The American Voice; The Antioch Review; Arts & Letters; Carolina Quarterly; Chelsea; Cimarron Review; Cincinnati Poetry Review; Crazyhorse; The Georgia Review; The Gettysburg Review; Ironwood; Luna; Memphis State Review; Mississippi Review; The Missouri Review; The

North American Review; The Ohio Review; Ploughshares; Poetry ("Bountiful," "The Conversion of Saint Paul," "Homo Sapiens," "Hummingbirds," "If I Die," "The Inarticulate," "The Mystery of the Caves," "'Night in the Tropics' (1858-59?)," "Not Just Any Death," "Not Love," "Paradys," "Pollen," "Preserves," "Reading Dickens," "Romance in the Old Folks' Home," "Scorpions," "Shhh"); *Poetry Ireland Review; Prairie Schooner; Seneca Review; Shenandoah; Southern Poetry Review; Three Rivers Poetry Journal; The World & I; The Yale Review.*

"The Mystery of the Caves" was reprinted in *The Pushcart Prize IX*. "Miles Weeping" was reprinted in *The Pushcart Prize XV*.

Some of the poems bear dedications: "Christ at the Apollo, 1962" to Andrew Hudgins; "Brooklyn Waterfall" to Stephen Dunn; "Preserves" to Hannelore Heyen; "Frank Sinatra" to Michael and Barbara Sheridan; "Lunch Hour" to Jody Swilky; "Snakes" to Mary Oliver; "Avesta" to T; "Not Love" to KH.

I want to express my gratitude to Yaddo, The MacDowell Colony, The Virginia Center for the Creative Arts, The Tyrone Guthrie Centre at Annaghmakerrig (Ireland), and The Anderson Center for Interdisciplinary Studies for residencies that allowed me to complete these poems.

Salisbury University, the SU Foundation, and the Fulton School of Liberal Arts at SU offered generous support, which enabled me to complete this book.

And to my mother, Dorothy, and my daughter, Kiernan, pure pleasure, I remain immeasurably grateful.

ABOUT THE AUTHOR

Michael Waters is Professor of English at Salisbury University on the Eastern Shore of Maryland. His previous volumes include *Green Ash, Red Maple, Black Gum* (BOA Editions, 1997), *Bountiful* (1992), *The Burden Lifters* (1989), *Anniversary of the Air* (1985)—these three titles from Carnegie Mellon University Press—*Not Just Any Death* (BOA Editions, 1979), and *Fish Light* (Ithaca House, 1975). Among his awards are a Fellowship in Creative Writing from the National Endowment for the Arts, several Individual Artist Awards from the Maryland State Arts Council, and two Pushcart Prizes. He has taught in the creative writing programs at Ohio University and the University of Maryland, and has been Visiting Professor of American Literature at the University of Athens, Greece, as well as Banister Writer-in-Residence at Sweet Briar College in Virginia. He lives in Salisbury with his wife, Mihaela Moscaliuc, and his daughter, Kiernan.

BOA EDITIONS, LTD.

AMERICAN POETS CONTINUUM SERIES

Vol. 1   *The Fuhrer Bunker: A Cycle
          of Poems in Progress*
          W. D. Snodgrass

Vol. 2   *She*
          M. L. Rosenthal

Vol. 3   *Living With Distance*
          Ralph J. Mills, Jr.

Vol. 4   *Not Just Any Death*
          Michael Waters

Vol. 5   *That Was Then: New and
          Selected Poems*
          Isabella Gardner

Vol. 6   *Things That Happen Where
          There Aren't Any People*
          William Stafford

Vol. 7   *The Bridge of Change:
          Poems 1974–1980*
          John Logan

Vol. 8   *Signatures*
          Joseph Stroud

Vol. 9   *People Live Here: Selected
          Poems 1949–1983*
          Louis Simpson

Vol. 10 *Yin*
          Carolyn Kizer

Vol. 11 *Duhamel: Ideas of Order in
          Little Canada*
          Bill Tremblay

Vol. 12 *Seeing It Was So*
          Anthony Piccione

Vol. 13 *Hyam Plutzik: The Collected
          Poems*

Vol. 14 *Good Woman: Poems and a
          Memoir 1969–1980*
          Lucille Clifton

Vol. 15 *Next: New Poems*
          Lucille Clifton

Vol. 16 *Roxa: Voices of the Culver
          Family*
          William B. Patrick

Vol. 17 *John Logan: The Collected Poems*

Vol. 18 *Isabella Gardner: The
          Collected Poems*

Vol. 19 *The Sunken Lightship*
          Peter Makuck

Vol. 20 *The City in Which I Love You*
          Li-Young Lee

Vol. 21 *Quilting: Poems 1987–1990*
          Lucille Clifton

Vol. 22 *John Logan: The Collected
          Fiction*

Vol. 23 *Shenandoah and Other Verse
          Plays*
          Delmore Schwartz

Vol. 24 *Nobody Lives on Arthur
          Godfrey Boulevard*
          Gerald Costanzo

Vol. 25 *The Book of Names: New and
          Selected Poems*
          Barton Sutter

Vol. 26 *Each in His Season*
          W. D. Snodgrass

Vol. 27 *Wordworks: Poems Selected
          and New*
          Richard Kostelanetz

Vol. 28 *What We Carry*
          Dorianne Laux

Vol. 29 *Red Suitcase*
          Naomi Shihab Nye

Vol. 30 *Song*
          Brigit Pegeen Kelly

Vol. 31 *The Fuehrer Bunker:
          The Complete Cycle*
          W. D. Snodgrass

Vol. 32 *For the Kingdom*
          Anthony Piccione

Vol. 33 *The Quicken Tree*
          Bill Knott

Vol. 34 *These Upraised Hands*
          William B. Patrick

Vol. 35 *Crazy Horse in Stillness*
          William Heyen

COLOPHON

Parthenopi: New and Selected Poems, by Michael Waters,
was set using Dante fonts, and Monotype Arabesque ornaments,
by Richard Foerster, York Beach, Maine. The jacket and cover
were designed by Daphne Poulin-Stofer, Rochester, New York.
Manufacturing was by McNaughton & Gunn, Saline, Michigan.

Special support for this book came from the following individuals:
Debra Audet, Joseph Bednarik & Liesl Slabaugh,
Bruce Bond, Richard Garth & Mimi Hwang,
Dane & Judy Gordon, Tom & Peggy Hubbard,
Robert & Willy Hursh, Archie & Pat Kutz,
John & Barbara Lovenheim, Francie & Robert Marx,
Boo Poulin, Deborah Ronnen,
Dona Dumitra Rosu, Pat & Michael Wilder.